The

CEO

Contract

Creating
a Winning
Partnership

Carrole A. Wolin, Editor

Yong Li & Kent A. Phillippe, Research

Stephen J. Hirschfeld & Pamela A. Humbert, Contributing Authors

Design & Layout by Desktop Design

Published by the Community College Press,
a division of the
American Association of Community Colleges
One Dupont Circle, NW, Suite 410
Washington, DC 20036-1176

Telephone: 202/728-0200
Fax: 202/833-2467
http://www.aacc.nche.edu

ISBN: 0-87117-300-X

TABLE OF CONTENTS

TABLES

GRAPHS

ABSTRACT

The CEO Contract: Creating a Winning Partnership reports on the findings of a 1995 survey of community college chief executive officers (CEOs) that examined various aspects of the CEO employment contract. This survey found that the majority of community college CEOs serve under a formal contract and that CEO compensation and benefits were closely associated with such variables as campus size and region. This work includes an informed discussion of the CEO contract, with a particular focus on the separation clause, by a legal expert. In this discussion, community colleges are advised to adopt comprehensive employment contracts for their CEOs that not only describe the terms and conditions of employment, but also the circumstances under which a CEO's services may be terminated so as to avoid potential litigation and to promote the general public good.

FOREWORD

The CEO Contract: Creating a Winning Partnership is sponsored by the Presidents Academy Executive Committee (see Appendix A) of the American Association of Community Colleges (AACC). This monograph has been prepared as a service to chief executive officers of AACC-member institutions in order to provide community college leaders with up-to-date comparative data and legal opinion on CEO employment contracts. A particular focus of this monograph is the separation clause and related issues.

The AACC Presidents Academy is the forum and voice of AACC-member CEOs. It was formally established in 1975 by the AACC Board of Directors to offer inservice programs that support the roles, welfare, and professional development of chief executive officers. The Presidents Academy also provides opportunities to exchange ideas and to express the views of AACC-member CEOs. Further, the purposes of the organization include serving chief executive officers, promoting institutions, and assisting AACC in fulfilling its goals.

The CEO Contract: Creating a Winning Partnership offers the following benefits to CEOs:

- A heightened awareness of the importance of well-developed contracts that include separation clauses,

- An increased knowledge of the types and scope of benefits that enhance an employment contract, and

- An increased ability on the part of CEOs to negotiate an employment contract.

> Membership in the Presidents Academy includes all CEOs of AACC-member institutions.
>
> A 13-member Executive Committee, elected annually by its members, governs the Academy. The Academy chair attends AACC Board of Directors meetings in a liaison capacity.
>
> The Executive Committee meets three times a year.

> ◊ **Presidents Academy members receive professional development opportunities by participating in programs sponsored annually by the Presidents Academy Executive Committee, including:**
>
> ☐ The Summer Experience
>
> ☐ The DC Experience
>
> ☐ Sessions for CEOs at the ACCT Convention
>
> ☐ Special forums, meetings, and workshops at the AACC Annual Convention

We wish to thank all members of the 1995–1996 Presidents Academy Executive Committee and especially Jo Anne McFarland and Martha Smith for launching this important initiative. Thanks also go to Stephen Hirschfeld, Tommy Lewis, Jr., Jo Anne McFarland, Ruth Mercedes Smith, and Carrole Wolin for communicating the important findings at two national conventions. No less important were the contributions of Kent Phillippe, Yong Li, and Pamela Humbert. Sincere thanks to our editors, Carrole Wolin and Robert Pedersen. In addition, special gratitude is extended to the chief executive officers who participated in and made this study possible.

Karen A. Bowyer

*President, Dyersburg State Community College
and Chair, Presidents Academy Executive Committee*

David R. Pierce

*President and CEO, American Association of
Community Colleges*

June 1996

A PERSPECTIVE ON THE CEO CONTRACT

S uccessful community college leadership requires tremendous dedication, focus, and professional expertise. As a natural consequence, the role of the CEO involves some risk. Leading a community college is no exception. Essential to minimizing this risk is a clear understanding and agreement about expectations between a college's governing board and its CEO. Where there is a clear understanding, the CEO can pour his or her energy into planning and positive action.

A well-crafted contract between a college board and CEO is one way—and possibly the best way—to ensure clear communication. A contract expresses the institution's values and the amount of flexibility allowed to the CEO. It also can serve as an effective recruitment tool.

The importance of the CEO contract is certain to grow in the near future. In an era when the tenure of presidents appears to be growing shorter, and pending CEO retirements likely will result in the appointment of many new presidents, the interest of a governing board in promoting CEO effectiveness will be best served when its expectations of the CEO are made clear and explicit from the outset. As Koltai has observed, "[H]andling the entrance correctly helps to ensure the strength of the presi-

The CEO Contract: Creating a Winning Partnership offers CEOs:

☐ A *heightened* awareness of the importance of well-developed contracts that include separation clauses

☐ An increased knowledge of the types and scope of benefits that enhance an employment contract

☐ An increased ability on the part of CEOs to negotiate an employment contract

dency" (Koltai, 1984). This monograph will provide guidance to both governing boards and CEOs in crafting contracts that will benefit them, and the communities they serve, over the course of their partnership.

CONTRACTS IN GENERAL

Each community college board of trustees must adapt its college's mission and operations to local economic, educational, and political conditions. Consequently, its expectations and its compensation of a CEO will be directly influenced by these conditions (Nicholson, 1981).

Indeed, given the great diversity among the communities served by community colleges, it should come as no surprise that, although every CEO has an employment contract of some form, CEO contracts vary greatly. Some are highly detailed and thorough; others are based on a handshake and are embodied in board policies. But regardless of its complexity, the CEO contract is central to the effectiveness of any community college. It represents the basic policy and the ground rules governing the CEO's relationship to his/her board and, in most states, represents the only tangible employment security protection a college CEO enjoys (Parnell & Rivera, 1991).

A good contract enhances a clear understanding of the nature and scope of the CEO–board relationship, thereby helping to establish a firm basis for its healthy development. Moreover, well-crafted contracts protect the interest of the governing board and the larger public in maintaining an accountable college leadership while providing direction and protection for the CEO.

> *"If good fences make good neighbors . . . then good contracts make good working relationships between the CEO and the board . . . . contribution, compensation, and expectations must be in balance if the relationship is to be productive. "*
>
> (Nicholson, 1988)

BASIC CONTRACT ELEMENTS

K ey elements of a comprehensive CEO contract include salary and other forms of compensation, a position description, provision for periodic review/evaluation, and conditions and provisions for contract termination (Koltai, 1984).

The contract preamble or introductory section typically consists of a limited number of "whereas" clauses used to explain the contract's purposes. The preamble is then followed by the "length" section, which sets the duration of the agreement. More contracts or letters specify three years or less than periods longer than three years, although a substantial number of CEO contracts are for five years. (Neff, 1994). A provision for extensions can be included. Some contracts now contain a "roll-over" provision. This allows the board to extend a contract without renegotiating every other provision (Parnell & Rivera, 1991).

> ◈
> ◐ In a 1986 survey, only 4 percent spelled out duties specifically. Most contracts refer to an attached job description or established policies as expressions of the duties to be performed.
>
> (Nicholson, 1988)

A 1994 Association of Governing Boards (AGB) study found that the percentage of CEOs with comprehensive contracts had declined from the percentage reported in a 1991 survey by the College and University Personnel Association (CUPA). The CUPA survey found 77 percent of the replying institutions had a contract with their presidents. However, the AGB analysis found that only 28 percent of college and university CEOs had comprehensive contracts. The others ranged from moderately detailed or incomplete to brief letters of appointment. All two-year institutions in the AGB survey used some form of contractual letter or other formal document (Neff, 1994).

Beyond duration, the CEO contract can address a number of other topics. Parnell and Rivera have recommended the inclusion of a brief statement of duties and responsibilities that describes the CEO's function and grants specific authority to the CEO (1991). Organizational issues—who reports to whom, and in what capacity—also might be considered (Nicholson, 1988). Appleberry (1996) provides a helpful checklist for CEO contracts (see Table 1).

One obvious element of a CEO contract is salary and other compensation (e.g., health care, housing, transportation, and deferred compensation). Further, a contract might include provisions for evaluation and conflict resolution, tenure, post-presidential provisions or employment, sabbatical leave, and ownership of files and documents (Neff, 1994). An increasingly important issue that should be addressed in a contract is the extent to which the CEO may consult, lecture, write, or hold other salaried positions outside the college (Parnell & Rivera, 1991).

More comprehensive contracts will typically contain some provision for suspension or termination, including what will happen if the president is ill or absent for a lengthy period or if termination for cause is required. Letters and brief contracts rarely incorporate such provisions (Neff, 1994).

COMPENSATION

Today's financial constraints necessitate careful consideration of all forms of compensation—both salary and benefits—when negotiating an employment contract. A CEO contract should specify the annual salary, both in writing and in figures, as well as when and how it will be changed. It also should spell out the CEO's other benefits.

> ◊
> **In 1990, 22 percent of CEO contracts contained an itemized list of duties.**
>
> (Parnell & Rivera, 1991)

Checklist for a President's Contract

When hiring a college president, the governing board and the prospective chief executive must agree on a wide range of terms of employment (Appleberry, 1988). The interests of all parties are best served when there is a clearly stated, written agreement on the conditions of employment. Simple letters of appointment alone, although common, leave much unstated and, thus, unclear to the governing board and the president alike. This is particularly true for the methods of exiting the presidency. At the time of presidential appointment, governing boards and presidents may not want to talk about the conditions of leaving the presidency, but such a time is probably the best one for reaching a mutually agreeable understanding and for lessening the possibility of institutional turmoil should the separation be controversial. Discussions between the president and the governing board should include at least the items listed below (Appleberry, 1996).

■ Nature, scope of authority, and responsibility vested in office of the president by the governing board

■ Conditions of employment
  • Length of appointment or contract
  • Time frame for renewal consideration, if appropriate
  • Academic rank
  • Academic tenure, or how obtained
  • The process and procedure to be followed for assessing the performance of the president, including any due-process procedures

■ Compensation
  • Base salary
  • Deferred compensation
    1. Purchase of annuity to limit of tax laws
    2. Amount held to be distributed at a future time, such as the end of tenure as president
  • Retirement plans
    1. Who pays

2. How much is contributed

3. Voluntary deduction for additional plans

4. Is the plan tied to Social Security

- Other sources of compensation (i.e., foundation support)
- Consulting opportunities
- Service on corporate and other paying boards
- Financial agreement upon leaving the presidency, whether leaving the campus or staying in a different role. Any long-range financial payments accrued during the presidency that are paid after separation from the institution should be spelled out

■ Insurance
- Health

1. Spouse

2. Dependents (to what age)

3. Major medical (to what limits)

4. Yearly medical examination

- Life
- Disability
- Professional liability: Bridge policy between personal and that purchased or provided by the institution
- Travel insurance (accidental death or disability)
- Automobile (institution owned) insurance: Does institutional insurance cover rental cars

■ Housing
- If housing is provided:

1. Which bills are paid by institution

2. Requirements regarding family vs. official use

3. Redecorating (how many dollars, who decides what)

4. Building addition (how many dollars, who decides what)

5. Lawn and grounds care

6. Maid and/or housekeeping service

7. Opportunities to acquire personal residential real estate

8. Replacement or repair of personally owned furniture

- If housing is not provided:
  1. Housing allowance
  2. Lawn and grounds care
  3. Housekeeping service
  4. Replacement or repair of personally owned furniture

■ Travel
- If a car is provided:
  1. What size
  2. What expenses
  3. What about personal use

- If car is not provided:
  1. Mileage reimbursement rate (mechanism for adjustment)
- Travel-related expenses to be covered
- Payment for spouse travel
- Attendance at meetings (what kind, how many, where)
- International travel

■ Leaves
- Vacation:
  1. Accrue at what rate
  2. Accumulated to what limit
  3. Payment for non-use or upon separation

- Sick:
  1. Accrue at what rate
  2. Accumulated to what limit
  3. Payment for non-use or upon separation

- Professional development:
  1. Length
  2. Salary
  3. Status upon return

■ Other considerations
- Social responsibilities
  1. How paid, and what limits
  2. Payment for off-campus and on-campus obligations

3. Who performs social coordinator responsibilities, and how remunerated

- Expectations by, for, and about spouse:
  1. Campus expectations
  2. Community expectations
  3. Extent of involvement with institution
  4. Outside employment
  5. Campus employment
  6. Secretarial and other support when conducting institutional business

- Entertainment expense—on and off campus
- Club dues
- Professional memberships
- Service on boards
- Acceptance of leadership positions (local, state, national)
- Research and writing assistance
- Tickets to institutional and noninstitutional events
- Moving expenses
- Financial counseling
- Family use of facilities and payment for services
  1. Tuition
  2. Babysitting
  3. Day care for minor children

■ Leaving the presidency
- Length of notice required by the president and/or the governing board
- Due-process requirements
- Position of responsibility if the president stays with the institution:
  1. How is salary determined
  2. Office, secretary, expense allowance, other perks
- Outplacement service
- Relocation expense
- Separation package, agreement or allowance
- Retraining opportunities (leave with pay, how long)

Excerpted from Appleberry, 1996,
The Presidential Search and Conditions of Employment.

SALARY

CEO salaries have risen steadily since 1981, when the average CEO earned about $48,400. By 1986, CEO mean salaries had risen 30 percent to nearly $62,950, and 1991 showed the national average to be nearly $79,800 (Parnell & Rivera, 1991).

The 1985–86 Peat Marwick/American School & University Compensation Survey of 133 institutions found a close correlation between college enrollment and CEO salary. As expected, the CEO base salary increased progressively with enrollment.

Other data also revealed wide regional differences in CEO salaries. For example, in 1990–91, California CEOs earned maximum salaries ranging from $95,000 to $119,700 (Creal & Beyer, 1995). In contrast, a 1992–93 survey showed that 29 percent of North Carolina CEOs received less than $79,981, while 40 percent received less than $88,011 (Vanderheyden, 1994).

> ◊ "Compensation and contribution must balance if relationships are to be equitable and effective."
>
> (Nicholson, 1988)

BENEFITS

At a minimum, a CEO should be granted all of the fringe benefits received by other college administrators. These benefits typically include health insurance, retirement, life insurance, and sick and personal leave (Parnell & Rivera, 1991).

Cars remain a common perquisite of CEOs. In 1990, 54 percent of those surveyed had a college-provided auto, while 24 percent were reimbursed for personal automobile use (Parnell & Rivera, 1991). Parnell and Rivera recommend that if a college-owned automobile is provided, insurance for the automobile, as well as a college gasoline credit card and vehicle maintenance, should be the responsibility of the college.

In 1985–86, more than 60 percent of CEOs received some form of retirement compensation. In 1986, retirement contributions ranged from 7.9 to 10.6 percent of base salary in community colleges (Peat Marwick/AS&U, 1986). A 1990 survey reported that 82 percent of CEO contracts provided for some form of life insurance, with some contracts allowing the CEO to retain group insurance benefits after retirement (Parnell & Rivera, 1991).

> ◈
> ◉　All issues
> should be checked
> against state
> statute.
>
> (Parnell & Rivera,
> 1991)

Professional development allowances and association memberships are provided to CEOs about equally, with the actual dollar value of these benefits depending upon the size of the college. In 1986, Peat Marwick/AS&U reported that more than a third of CEOs—an 18 percent increase over the previous year—received professional development allowances by contract. In 1990, 45 percent of community college CEO contracts provided for professional dues payment by the college. However, provision for payment of association dues is often contingent upon state law (Parnell & Rivera, 1991).

Nearly 60 percent of all institutions allow CEOs the opportunity to earn outside income (Peat Marwick/AS&U, 1986). Professional liability coverage must accord with state law, and only 9 percent of 1990 CEOs have a professional liability clause in their contracts (Parnell & Rivera, 1991).

CEO contracts also may include other special benefits. One such is a deferred income or severance pay plan in combination with a salary and life insurance plan. In a 1990 survey, 10 percent of CEOs reported having a deferred or severance pay provision in their contract, while 16 percent indicated that their college provided other retirement benefits beyond the usual retirement plan (Parnell & Rivera, 1991). In a 1990 survey, 30 percent of CEO contracts provided for some form of sabbatical leave, usually after seven years of service (Parnell & Rivera, 1991). Loans and financial planning are not widely offered as perquisites, while supplemental life insurance programs were reported by more than 36 percent of the respondents (Peat Marwick/AS&U, 1986).

While 26 percent of CEOs receive some form of housing benefit, smaller institutions are more likely to offer this perquisite than are colleges with 2,500 or more students (Peat Marwick/AS&U, 1986).

While 33 percent listed a physical exam as a benefit, only about 20 percent of 1990 responses showed provision of some type of disability insurance, and just 18 percent had clauses providing for a college-paid annual physical examination (Parnell & Rivera, 1991).

Occasionally, spouse travel and/or dependent tuition may be included in a contract. Smaller institutions provide dependent tuition more often than larger ones. (Peat Marwick/AS&U, 1986).

EVALUATION AND SEPARATION

Absent of specific board action, such as a notice of nonrenewal, most CEO contracts are extended automatically (Nicholson, 1988). Parnell and Rivera (1991) have recommended that CEO contracts include some provision for adequate notice of renewal to permit the CEO sufficient time to look for other employment if a board elects not to renew the contract. Some multi-year contracts already provide notice of six to 12 months in advance of renewal or termination.

> ◆
> ● *Annual
> contract renewal
> in 1991 was 49
> percent. This 1995
> survey revealed
> an increase to 51
> percent.*

EVALUATION

In a 1990 survey, 65 percent of CEO contracts required a periodic—most often annual—performance review. Consistent with current management theory, mutual involvement in the CEO evaluation process has become the rule. Many institutions specifically require evaluation of both the CEO and governing board to assess accomplishments and improve performance (Parnell & Rivera, 1991).

In North Carolina, for example, the North Carolina State Board of Community Colleges has adopted a formal procedure for evaluation of college presidents in an effort to improve the quality of that state's community college system and to stimulate the leadership and productivity of the system's presidents. Through this process, the system's board expects to:

- Close the gap between presidential authority and accountability,
- Ensure that the CEO and the board have mutually agreed-upon goals for the college,
- Identify strengths and weaknesses of the president and the college, and
- Define the scope and role of the office and the president's performance in it (Dowdy, 1987).

SEPARATION

In 1988, Nicholson found that 25 percent of CEO contracts contained a provision for board-initiated termination, up from 10 percent in 1981. Almost all of these contracts included termination for cause, including provision for automatic termination in the case of serious misconduct. One contract cited "ignoring" board policy as a cause for dismissal. Release in the case of CEO incapacitation often was addressed. Some contracts required that the board state reasons for dismissal, while others clearly stated that no reasons are to be given and no recourse would be available to the terminated CEO (Nicholson, 1988).

As a general rule, termination provisions are divided into different categories. The most prevalent are "no fault" and "due cause."

- **No fault.** This provision in essence outlines the ability of either side to terminate employment relationships at will, without having to set forth a specific justification for the termination decision. When a CEO is terminated "without fault" or at will under an employment contract, typically the most generous severance payments allowed for under the contract are granted. This is because no specific cause or justification for the termination is outlined, but instead the decision is made at the pleasure of the college.

- **Due cause.** This provision typically sets forth with specificity the circumstances under which a CEO can be terminated. The most prevalent reasons set forth for a due cause termination include significant performance problems or serious misconduct. When this provision is exercised, due process standards should be followed. These include providing notice of the problem(s) with an opportunity to be heard, and an opportunity to correct and/or explain the behavior in question.

> ◊ *"In any event, there should be an understanding that any action taken on renewal or nonrenewal is the result of a conscious decision by both the college board and the CEO and never because of default.*
>
> (Parnell & Rivera, 1991)

Where a CEO is terminated for due cause, typically less severance pay is afforded. In some contracts, when a CEO is terminated for due cause, no severance pay is provided. That is something subject to negotiation between the parties.

Parnell and Rivera (1991) also have argued that the CEO contract should include the right to a due process hearing before the college board when the CEO disputes a termination. At a minimum, they called for:

- Written notice of the reasons the contract is being terminated;
- The CEO's right to appear before the college board in closed executive session or public hearing, at the option of the CEO;
- The CEO's right to representation at any hearing;
- The right to a written decision summarizing the findings of the hearing; and
- An indication that neither the college board nor the CEO waives any right either party might have affecting the contract under state or federal law.

Contract Provision for Separation

While the current literature addresses many issues involved in CEO termination, the separation clause in CEO contracts largely has been ignored. In recognition of this fact, the AACC Presidents Academy authorized a study of CEO contracts to gather and analyze information on CEO contracts and their inclusion of separation clauses.

A significant number of CEO separations are not wholly voluntary and often prove a wrenching experience for all parties. Certainly, stories of bad termination experiences abound in college circles. Ness and Miller (1988) assert that "most often, the fault may be traced to the time of the initial appointment, when neither the president nor board had learned enough about the character and expectations of the other."

Some might question the wisdom of incorporating into a CEO contract specific provision for separation. However, the basic premise underlying the inclusion of a separation clause is to provide both parties with the tools to manage conflict. The ability to address termination at the outset of the contract often indicates a desire for open communication and an ability to face difficult issues squarely by both the board and CEO. Conflict resolution, rather than conflict suppression, becomes the goal. While not all issues of potential misunderstanding can be settled in an employment contract—written board policies and collective bargaining contracts also may guide action (Parnell & Rivera, 1991)—a separation clause provides the parties with a mechanism by which they can "agree to disagree." Further, a separation clause, thought out calmly ahead of time, can help minimize the effects of anger and disillusionment that can arise during a stressful process.

> "A carefully planned and written contract describes the relationship both parties desire and avoids unexpected surprises."
>
> (Parnell & Rivera, 1991)

Clearly, both community college boards and their CEOs can benefit when separation clauses are an integral part of their contract.

Carrole A. Wolin is Director of Professional Development at the American Association of Community Colleges, Washington, DC.

Pamela A. Humbert, a publications and design consultant, is owner of DESKTOP DESIGN in Silver Spring, Maryland.

SURVEY RESULTS

The American Association of Community Colleges (AACC) Presidents Academy Executive Committee conducted a survey of CEO contracts, with a particular focus on separation provisions, during Fall 1995. The survey instrument was mailed to all 1,046 CEOs of AACC-member colleges. Initially, 364 CEOs responded, while an additional 253 CEOs responded to a follow-up mailing. A total of 617 CEOs responded, giving an overall participation rate of 59 percent. Table 2 provides a list of terms used in the survey analysis and the number of respondents per category.

Responses were received from CEOs representing all types of accredited two-year institutions, both public and private, including single-campus colleges, multi-campus colleges, colleges of multi-college districts, and district offices. The respondents also mirrored the diversity of CEOs in virtually all respects, as reflected by Table 3.

> ◈ *To obtain information on the survey results, method of analysis, or for a copy of the survey instrument, contact the research department at AACC, One Dupont Circle, NW, Suite 410, Washington, DC 20036-1176*

ANALYSIS OF CONTRACT ELEMENTS

Consistent with previous studies, this survey found that a substantial majority—about three-fourths—of community college CEOs worked under a formal contract. However, of those CEOs with a formal contract, fewer than half had contracts that included a separation clause. Of CEOs without a formal contract, most, at slightly more than 80 percent, did not consider the lack of formal contract a problem.

TERMS AND NUMBER OF RESPONDENTS PER CATEGORY

CONTRACT STATUS — Three categories:

With no formal contract	150
With formal contract but no separation clause	258
With formal contract and separation clause	209

PROBLEM WITH NO CONTRACT — *Whether lack of a formal contract was a problem. Applies only to those with no formal contract:*

Yes	25	No	109

LENGTH OF CONTRACT — *Applies to those with a formal contract:*

1-year contract	107
2-year contract	50
3-year contract	209
4-year contract	51
5-year contract	32
No length specified	19
Other	20

FREQUENCY OF RENEWAL — *How frequently the contract is reviewed and renewed:*

Renewed once a year	309
Renewed every one to three years	39
Renewed after more than three years	70

REQUIRE "DUE CAUSE" — *Does the separation clause require "Due Cause"?*

Yes	163	No	48

PROVIDE "NO FAULT" — *Does the separation clause provide for "No Fault" separation?*

Yes	100	No	108

REGION — *Five categories for geographical regions:*

Central	136	Southern	159
Northern	99	Western	96
Pacific	106		

See Appendix B for a list of respondents per state by region.

BENEFITS — *Combined to form three categories:*

Supplemental: including house provided, housing allowance, vehicle provided, and vehicle allowance.

Insurance/annuity: including health insurance, life insurance, and tax-sheltered annuity.

Development: including professional development-related benefits such as travel allowance, professional dues, staff/secretary support, office/space use, and other professional-related benefits.

————————————————————————————————————TABLE 3

DEMOGRAPHIC CHARACTERISTICS OF RESPONDENTS

Demographic Characteristics	Percentages/Averages
Male	82.2
Female	16.8
Average Age	54.0
Non-Hispanic White	68.0
Other Racial Groups	8.7
African American	6.5
Hispanic	3.6
Native American	2.6
Asian/Pacific Islander	1.5
Public	93.5
Private	2.9
Single-Campus College	58.2
Multi-Campus College	30.5
College of Multi-College District	7.5
District Office of College of Multi-College District	3.6

Approximately 60 percent of CEO contracts were for three years or less. One in five CEO contracts were for one year, while two-fifths were for three years. CEOs with separation clauses also tended to have longer contracts than those without separation clauses. The average contract length for those with and without separation clauses, respectively, was three years and two-and-a-half years (see Graph 1).

Three out of four CEOs had their contracts reviewed or renewed annually, even though many of these contracts were for longer than a year. Whether the contract required a separation clause was not related to the frequency of the review or renewal of the contract. For those contracts with a separation

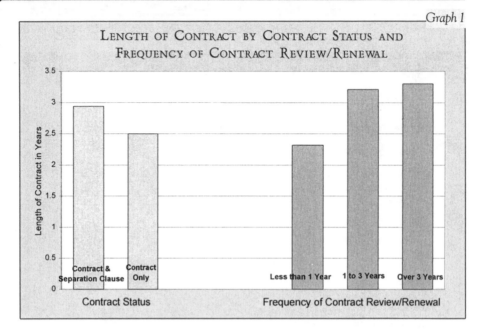

Graph 1

LENGTH OF CONTRACT BY CONTRACT STATUS AND FREQUENCY OF CONTRACT REVIEW/RENEWAL

clause, the frequency of renewal also was unrelated to whether the separation clause required due cause or provided for no fault. However, as expected, the longer the contract, the less frequently it was reviewed (see Graph 1). About 77 percent of the separation clauses required due cause. Further, longer contracts that included a separation clause were more likely to require due cause. For those requiring due cause, the average length of contract was three years, while it was about two-and-a-half years for those not requiring due cause.

ANALYSIS OF BENEFITS

CEOs received a number of benefits. Supplemental benefits averaged 1.1 per contract, with insurance/annuity benefits at 2.0 and professional development-related benefits at 2.5. The three types of benefits were positively related—CEOs with one type of benefit also were more likely to receive the other two types. For specific items under each heading, see Benefits in Table 2.

Importantly, benefits did not seem to be used to compensate for a lower salary. CEOs with higher salaries received more benefits, while CEOs with lower salaries received fewer (see Graph 2).

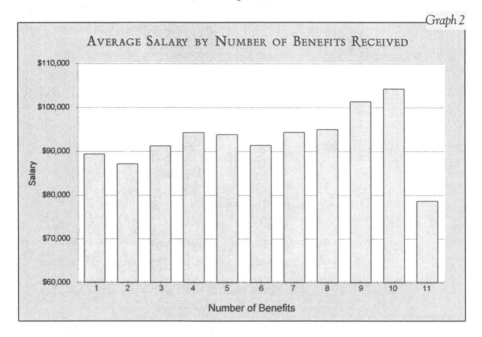

Graph 2

Neither the contract status of the CEO nor the frequency of contract review/renewal had an observable impact on benefits. However, both insurance and supplemental benefits were related to contract length and whether the separation clause required due cause. CEOs with longer contracts tended to have more insurance/annuity and supplemental benefits than those with shorter contracts. Further, CEOs whose separation clauses required due cause were more likely to enjoy greater insurance/annuity benefits, while CEOs whose separation clauses did

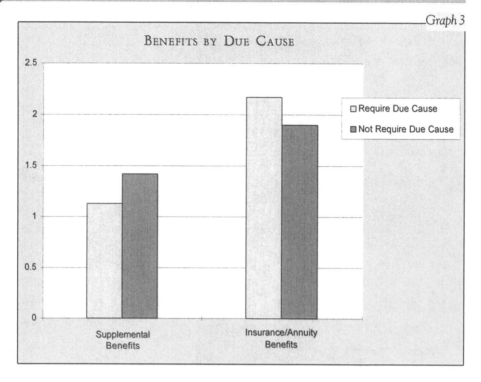

Graph 3

not require due cause were more likely to have above average supplemental benefits (see Graph 3).

One particularly interesting finding that emerged from this study reflected on the minority of CEOs who had no formal contract. Those CEOs who did not have a contract rated their situation as more acceptable if the college compensated them with higher supplemental benefits, such as housing and a car.

A similar finding of note had to do with salary. Salary was strongly related with contract status and length of contract. CEOs with a contract had a higher average salary ($93,659) than those without ($88,458), while CEOs with both a contract and a separation clause had even higher average salaries ($96,860) than those without a separation clause (see Graph 4). Longer contracts also were accompanied by higher salary, while CEOs with a shorter contract were more likely to have a lower salary (see Graph 4). However, salary was not related to either the frequency of contract provision for review/

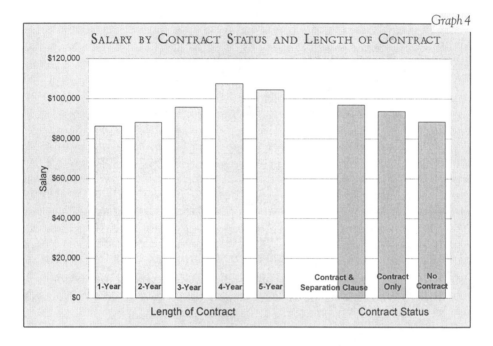

Graph 4

SALARY BY CONTRACT STATUS AND LENGTH OF CONTRACT

renewal or the frequency of separation clauses that required due cause or no fault separations.

ANALYSIS OF INSTITUTIONAL CHARACTERISTICS AND CONTRACTS

S urvey results indicated that type of institution had a significant impact on several features of CEO contracts. The comprehensiveness of the contract was related closely to the type of institution at which the CEO worked (see Graph 5). The data suggested that CEOs at district offices had relatively

Graph 5

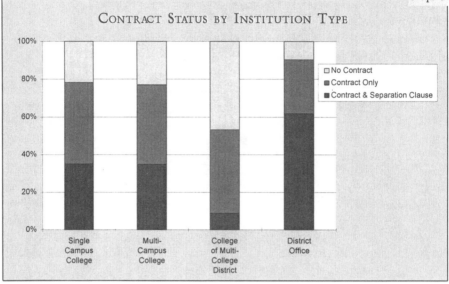

"safer" contracts (in that they were more likely to include separation clauses) than CEOs of colleges within a multi-college district. While the overall length of a contract does not appear to be influenced by the type of institution, both the frequency of review and the requirement to show due cause did. In the case of review frequency, it is interesting to note that CEOs of colleges in multi-campus districts were far more likely to face review only every three years than district office CEOs (see Graph 6).

ANALYSIS OF ENROLLMENT AND CONTRACTS

Two separate analyses of enrollment size were conducted. The uneven distribution of enrollments required that statistical corrections be made to enrollment size. Analyses were conducted using both the reported enrollment

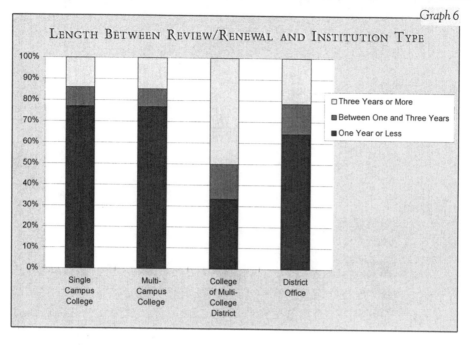

Graph 6

LENGTH BETWEEN REVIEW/RENEWAL AND INSTITUTION TYPE

□ Three Years or More
■ Between One and Three Years
■ One Year or Less

numbers and the statistically corrected enrollment figures. The results of both sets of analyses provided nearly identical results. Therefore, the results of the more conservative analysis, using statistically corrected enrollment, are reported here.

Consistent with the finding of earlier studies, college size had a significant impact on both the length of contract and CEO salaries. The relationship between salary and college size was straightforward—the larger the college, the greater the salary. Although the relationship between enrollment and length of contract was not quite as straightforward (see Graph 7), for the most part, the smaller the enrollment, the shorter the contract tended to be. It should be noted that the two largest colleges included in the survey offered only a one-year CEO contract.

Graph 7

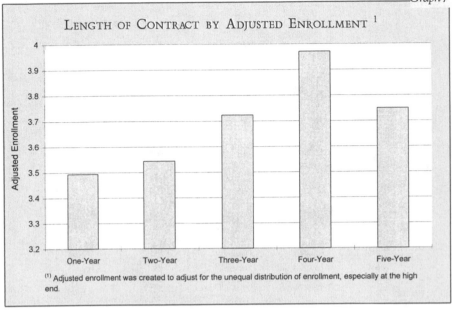

LENGTH OF CONTRACT BY ADJUSTED ENROLLMENT [1]

(1) Adjusted enrollment was created to adjust for the unequal distribution of enrollment, especially at the high end.

ANALYSIS OF CEO CHARACTERISTICS AND CONTRACTS

While the study found that institutional characteristics had an impact on many contract features, CEO characteristics had relatively little impact on contract variables, including benefits. Only contract length and contract comprehensiveness varied by CEO characteristics.

Length of contract was related to CEO age, years as a CEO in higher education, and years as a CEO at the current institution (see Graph 8). As a rule, CEOs with no formal contract were younger than those with formal contracts.

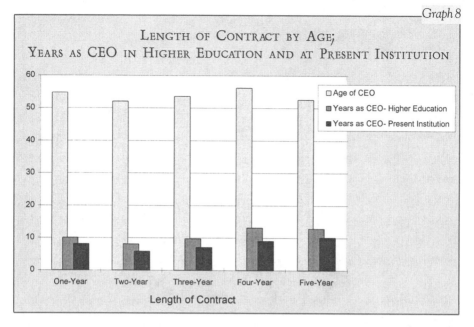

_____Graph 8

LENGTH OF CONTRACT BY AGE;
YEARS AS CEO IN HIGHER EDUCATION AND AT PRESENT INSTITUTION

□ Age of CEO
▨ Years as CEO- Higher Education
■ Years as CEO- Present Institution

Length of Contract

REGIONAL ANALYSIS OF
BENEFITS AND CONTRACTS

The community colleges that responded to the survey were separated into five geographic regions—Central, Northern, Pacific, Southern, and Western (see Appendix B)—for purposes of analysis. CEOs in the Pacific region were not only the most likely to have contracts, with fewer than 10 percent reporting no contract, they were also the most likely to have contracts that included separation clauses (see Graph 9).

Striking differences existed across the five regions with respect to both salary and benefits. Salaries tended to be higher in the Northern and Central regions, while they tended to be lowest in

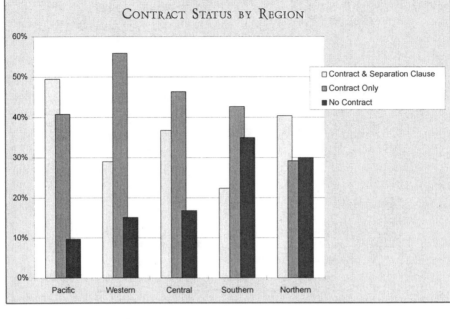

Graph 9

CONTRACT STATUS BY REGION

the Western region (see Graph 10). In part, this pattern may be due to the smaller average college size in the Western region. In addition, the number

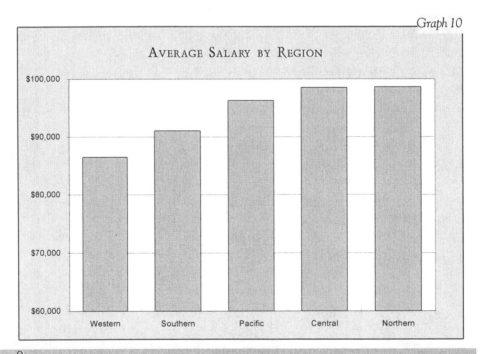

Graph 10

AVERAGE SALARY BY REGION

of benefits provided to CEOs varied across the five regions (see Graph 11). While the number of professional development benefits received by CEOs showed no difference across the five regions, the number of benefits received in the two other categories varied significantly. CEOs in Western and Northern regions tended to receive more supplemental benefits, while CEOs in the Pacific region were likely to receive fewer. Insurance/annuity benefits were most likely to be offered to CEOs in the Central and Northern regions, and least likely in the Southern region.

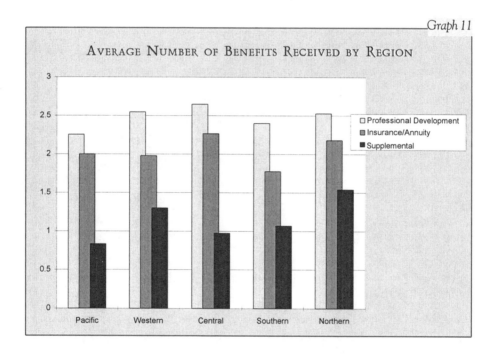

Graph 11

AVERAGE NUMBER OF BENEFITS RECEIVED BY REGION

☐ Professional Development
▨ Insurance/Annuity
■ Supplemental

ANALYSIS OF THE INTERACTION OF BENEFITS AND SALARY

It was hypothesized that salary and benefits might be differentially used as a means of compensating CEOs; therefore, the interaction of these two variables needed to be tested. To test this assumption, several multivariate analyses of salary and total benefits with institutional and individual characteristics were made to see if there were any interaction between these variables. As indicated in the "Analysis of Benefits" section, these two variables were positively related—as salary increased, CEOs tended to have more total benefits.

For most of the institutional and personal characteristics, no significant interactions between salary and benefits existed. CEOs at the low end of the salary range showed a slight tendency to receive more benefits the longer they had been a CEO in higher education. CEOs at the high end of the salary range tended to receive fewer benefits the longer they had been a CEO in higher education. There also was an interesting interaction between salary and benefits within the Southern region. At lower salary ranges, CEOs in the Southern region were more likely to receive benefits than CEOs in other regions. At the higher salary ranges, CEOs in the Southern region were less likely to receive benefits than CEOs in other regions. This finding suggests that colleges in the Southern region are more likely to use benefits as an incentive in lieu of salary for CEOs.

SUMMARY

In summary, the findings of this survey are not surprising. Having a formal contract does benefit CEOs significantly. A longer contract also was generally accompanied with less frequency of review/ renewal, along with higher salary and a greater likelihood for the inclusion of a "due cause" separation clause. Receiving a higher salary and one type of benefit also increased the probability that CEOs would receive other types of benefits.

Major differences in CEO contract provisions were noted, particularly when respondents were differentiated by region. CEOs from the Western region generally received lower-than-average salaries, while CEOs from the Southern region appear to receive a higher-than-average number of benefits in lieu of salary.

Table 4 on the following page highlights the most notable findings in this survey of CEO separation agreements and other elements of an employment contract.

Yong Li is Research Assistant and Kent A. Phillippe is Research Associate at the American Association of Community Colleges, Washington, DC.

TABLE 4

SUMMARY OF FINDINGS

■ CEOs with a separation clause had a longer contract than those with no separation clause.

■ The longer the contract, the less frequently the contract was reviewed/renewed and the more likely for the separation clause to require due cause.

■ Benefits that CEOs received were positively correlated with each other. Receiving one type of benefit increased the possibility of receiving other benefits as well.

■ As salary increased, so did the likelihood of more total benefits. Benefits and salary also tended to increase with the length of contract.

■ CEOs with more supplemental benefits tended to have less of a problem with lack of a formal contract.

■ CEOs with a formal contract had higher salaries than CEOs with no formal contract. The salary level was even higher for CEOs with a separation clause in their contract.

■ The type of institution influenced CEO contracts.

■ College size had a significant impact on both contract length and salaries.

■ Contract length was strongly related to the age of the CEOs, the number of years as a CEO in higher education, and how long the CEO had been at that institution.

■ Salaries tended to be higher in Northern and Central regions and lower in the Western region.

■ While CEOs in Western and Northern regions received more physical benefits, CEOs in the Pacific region received fewer.

■ Insurance/annuity benefits were most likely offered to CEOs in the Central and Northern regions and least likely in the Southern region.

■ Colleges in the Southern region were more likely to use benefits as an incentive in lieu of salary for CEOs.

A LEGAL PERSPECTIVE

CEO EMPLOYMENT CONTRACTS

I t was not so long ago that most chief executive officers, including community college presidents, were hired based on a handshake or, at most, a simple offer letter. But times have changed. We live in an increasingly litigious society. Today, when things go wrong in the employment setting and presidents are terminated or quit, both sides are increasingly looking to the judicial system to resolve their disputes. In addition, individuals who are being considered for presidential appointments are much more prone to want a specific and detailed understanding of the terms and conditions of their job before deciding whether to accept the position. Given these realities, it has become increasingly important for community colleges to develop and utilize employment contracts for their executives.

AN OVERVIEW

T he most common issues that need to be addressed in presidential employment contracts include: a description of the CEO's duties and responsibilities; a detailed list of the compensation and benefits to be provided, including how pay increases and bonuses will be awarded; the term of the appointment, and how that term can be extended or cut short; and the circumstances under which the CEO can be terminated and the conse-quences of that decision (e.g., notice period, reasons for termination, or termination payments).

> ◈ "A carefully planned and written contract describes the relationship both parties desire and avoids unexpected surprises."
> (Parnell & Rivera, 1991)

It is an old adage that "expectations are ninety-nine percent of an individual's satisfaction." In other words, if you raise someone's expectations to a certain level and then fail to meet them, that person will never be satisfied. An employment contract is designed so that both sides understand their mutual expectations and obligations. The document can and should be written in plain English so that both sides understand its terms and conditions. It also should be carefully crafted so that all key points with respect to the terms and conditions of the executive's job are covered. Once the contract has been written, an "integration" clause should be included in order to make certain that the document represents the *entire* understanding of the parties and that it supersedes all prior representations and agreements, both written and oral. This alleviates the possibility of misunderstandings based upon oral promises and side commitments that can occur, particularly during the recruiting and interviewing process.

Particular care must be taken in determining the circumstances under which the executive will be discharged prior to the end of his or her term. Ideally, there should be two forms of termination: termination for cause and termination without cause. If the executive is terminated for cause, no severance pay is typically provided. When the executive is terminated without cause (as, for example, when there is a change in the direction of the Board or the college's mission) severance pay and other benefits are normally provided. If the termination provision is properly written, the only issue to be decided is whether the college terminated the president with or without justification, as that term is defined by the contract. Courts will typically honor the contract and limit any damages to those required by the contract.

Litigation surrounding the termination of a community college president is time consuming and expensive. Perhaps even more importantly, it generates a lot of publicity that can adversely impact both the institution and the individual. Typically, it is in everyone's best interest for the executive to depart on as amicable a basis as possible and, where disputes arise, to have those disputes resolved in as confidential a manner as possible. To resolve disputes efficiently, confidentially, and in a cost-effective manner, community colleges should consider putting into their employment agreements a final and binding arbitration provision. Under such a provision, *all* disputes, whether based upon wrongful termination, breach of contract, discrimination, or any other tort or statutory claim, are resolved on a binding basis before a neutral arbitrator. Great care must be given to how this provision is written to ensure that the clause is enforceable and that it covers all possible disputes surrounding the executive's employment and termination. This provision should be written in a balanced way so that neither party is perceived as having an undue advantage going into arbitration. In essence, the only thing that should change is the forum for the dispute. All rights and remedies available to each side in court should remain available in arbitration.

Sample I and Sample II are examples of executive employment agreements. The first offers a model agreement that is geared specifically for higher education executives. Sample II is intended for the non-academic setting. While not geared to higher education, this second document offers a range of provisions that community colleges should consider adding to their CEO employment contracts. Table 5 provides a checklist for CEO employment contracts.

CHECKLIST FOR A CEO's EMPLOYMENT CONTRACT

■ Parties

■ Duties
  □ Work as Chief Executive Officer of the Institution
    • Tenure, no tenure, or credit toward tenure
  □ Run Institution under auspices of the Governing Board
  □ Suggest regulations, rules, and procedures for successful operation of the Institution
  □ Responsibilities
    • Fund raising, development, public and alumni relations
    • Institutional, faculty, and educational leadership
    • Long-range planning; formulating the budget; supervision of Institution buildings, grounds, and equipment; administration of the affairs of the Institution as best serves the Institution consistent with the Board policy
    • Student recruitment and services; faculty recruitment
    • Appointing, supervising, promoting, and dismissing staff members
  □ Devote full time, attention, and energy to Institution; no other gainful employment, except as expressly authorized (e.g., author, lecturer)
  □ Entertaining and travel
  □ Reasonable time for other voluntary activities (e.g., board, charity) provided that time commitment is not unreasonable

■ Term
  □ Contract commencement and termination dates
  □ Renewal at Board's option

■ Termination
  □ For just cause
    • Bases
      ✓ Deliberate or serious violation of Presidential duties
      ✓ Unwillingness to perform duties in good faith and to the best of ability

✓ Violation of any other terms or conditions of Agreement not remedied after thirty days' written notice

       ✓ Conduct that constitutes moral turpitude, or that would tend to bring public disrespect, contempt, or ridicule to the Institution

       ✓ A deliberate or serious violation of any law, rule, regulation, constitutional provision or bylaw of the Institution that, in the sole judgment of the Institution, reflects adversely upon the Institution

       ✓ Prolonged absence from duty without the Institution's consent

- President must first receive notice and an opportunity to be heard
- Institution's obligation to provide consideration ceases
- Institution not liable for President's loss of any other income, benefits, perquisites from any sources

☐ Termination without cause by Institution

- Death or permanent total disability
- Incapacity for six[1] months, as decided by medical doctor of Board's choice
- Institution must give _____ days' written notice
- President entitled to liquidated damages of:
  - ✓ An amount equal to _____ months of the President's salary
    - ◆ To be paid monthly over the remainder of the term of the Agreement
- President entitled to continue health insurance and group life insurance at own expense for up to eighteen months or longer if required by law
- Institution not liable for loss of any collateral business opportunities, perquisites, or income from any sources
- President obligated to mitigate Institution's obligation by making reasonable and diligent efforts to obtain employment which, once procured, ends Institution's obligation to pay liquidated damages
- Reassignment at full salary
- No Institution liability

☐ Termination without cause by President

- Institution entitled to _____ months of damages for each month of less than six months' notice

[1]Editor's Note: This particular provision may be subject to State law requirements.

- Compensation
  - ☐ Salary ($ _____ per year), payable *biweekly*, subject to applicable taxes
    - Salary reviewed annually
  - ☐ Must participate in retirement plan
  - ☐ Deferred compensation
  - ☐ Fringe benefits
    - Basic health insurance
    - Major medical insurance
    - [Dental insurance]
    - Life insurance
    - Payments in event of disability, total and partial
      - ✓ $_____ annual paid contributions to retirement plan
        - ◆ _____ % employer and _____ % employee
    - Presidential housing
    - Entertainment/business expense allowance (with or without documentation)
    - Car
    - Club membership dues (& charges)
    - Sick leave time (to _____ weeks per year)
    - Travel and travel-related expenses
    - Workers' Compensation
  - ☐ Vacation (two days/month of employment, not including holidays, up to _____ days per year)
  - ☐ Sabbatical
  - ☐ Income tax liabilities paid by President
- Entire agreement
- Modification of contract
  - ☐ By writing only
- Severability
- Waiver of breach
- Governing law
- Date and signatures of parties

LEGAL SCRUTINY OF BINDING ARBITRATION AGREEMENTS

When the U.S. Supreme Court in 1991 applied an arbitration provision in a securities employment agreement to an age discrimination claim in *Gilmer v. Interstate/ Johnson Lane Corp.*, 500 U.S. 20, the door appeared to have opened for employers in non-union settings to require their employees to agree to arbitrate employment disputes in lieu of litigation. This prospect was appealing. Experience shows that arbitration is less expensive than litigation and that employers fare better with arbitrators than with juries. But three decisions in unrelated cases, issued within a five-day period in December 1994 by different panels of judges of the federal Ninth Circuit Court of Appeals in California, reflect judicial concerns about applying arbitration provisions in ways that impinge upon other statutory and contractual rights.

Prudential Insurance Co. of America v. Lai,
42 F.3d 1299 (9th Cir. Dec. 20, 1994)

In *Lai*, the plaintiffs were two Prudential sales representatives. When they applied for these positions, they were required to sign a form known as a "U-4" containing an agreement "to arbitrate any dispute, claim or controversy that . . . is required to be arbitrated under the rules, constitutions, or bylaws of the organizations with which I register." These plaintiffs registered with the National Association of

Securities Dealers (NASD), which requires that disputes "arising in connection with the business" of members be arbitrated. According to the plaintiffs, arbitration was never mentioned when they were filling out Prudential's forms, and they were never given a copy of the NASD Manual, which contained the actual arbitration agreement.

When the plaintiffs sued Prudential in state court alleging sexual harassment and discrimination, Prudential obtained an order in federal court compelling the plaintiffs to arbitrate their claims. On appeal of that order, the Ninth Circuit noted that the issue was *not* whether an employee could ever agree to arbitrate a statutory claim. The Supreme Court in *Gilmer* said they can. The issue here was whether these particular employees had entered into a binding arbitration agreement and thereby waived their judicial remedies for violation of various state statutes. The Ninth Circuit said no. The Court found that "Congress intended there to be at least a knowing agreement to arbitrate employment disputes before an employee may be deemed to have waived the comprehensive statutory rights, remedies and procedural protections prescribed in Title VII and related state statutes."

In *Prudential*, these plaintiffs "could not have understood that in signing [the U-4 form], they were agreeing to arbitrate sexual discrimination suits." The Court noted that the U-4 form did not identify the kinds of disputes to be arbitrated. Even the NASD arbitration clause did not refer to employment disputes.

Graham Oil Co. v. ARCO Products Co.,

No. 92-35007, 1994 WL 701315 (9th Cir. Dec. 16, 1994)

Graham Oil was a distributor of ARCO gasoline in Oregon. Their relationship was governed by the Petroleum Marketing Practices Act (PMPA), a federal statute that protects certain rights of franchisees. Graham Oil's contract with ARCO contained an arbitration clause, which also included a waiver of certain statutory rights conferred upon franchisees by the PMPA. When ARCO notified Graham Oil of its intent to terminate the agreement, Graham Oil sued ARCO in federal district court. The district court ruled that arbitration was Graham Oil's sole remedy and dismissed the case.

On appeal, the Ninth Circuit reversed, finding the arbitration clause was invalid because it forfeited Graham Oil's rights under the PMPA to punitive damages, attorney's fees, and a one-year statute of limitations. The Court made an important distinction. Had the arbitration provision simply reflected an agreement "to substitute one legitimate dispute resolution forum for another" without a "surrender of statutory protections or benefits," the provision would have been valid. But this provision went further. It required Graham Oil to waive its statutorily-mandated rights under the PMPA, which was enacted by Congress to shield franchisees from the gross disparity of bargaining power enjoyed by franchisers. In so doing, the provision violated the PMPA.

Tracer Research Corp. v. National
Environmental Services Co.,
42 F.3d 1292 (9th Cir. Dec. 19, 1994)

Tracer Research sued National Environmental for various torts related to National Environmental's alleged misappropriation of trade secrets. Tracer had licensed a chemical process to National Environmental, and the license contained an arbitration clause that provided that "[i]n the event any controversy or claim arising out of this Agreement cannot be settled by the parties . . . such controversy or claim shall be settled by arbitration." In the trial court, National Environmental obtained an order referring the case to arbitration. On appeal, the Ninth Circuit reversed. The Court's reading of the arbitration clause should send lawyers every-where scurrying back to their word processors to check their boilerplate provisions. According to the Court, Tracer's tort claims did not "arise out of" the licensing agreement. Had that arbitration provision referred to claims "arising out of *or relating to*" the license agreement, the result would be different. In the Court's words, "[t]he omission of the 'relating to' language is 'significant.' "

LESSONS TO BE LEARNED

What is going on here? These judges were performing a balancing act. On the one hand, judges wish to encourage parties to arbitrate rather than litigate their claims. But there are two "other hands." First, arbitration is a matter of agreement between the parties, and these judges were uncomfortable that parties were being required to arbitrate matters they had not consciously agreed to arbitrate, like the plaintiffs in *Prudential* and *Tracer*. The second "other hand" is that the law recognizes that certain parties, like the franchisee-plaintiff in *Graham Oil*, lack bargaining power, and are given statutory rights to protect them that are not to be abridged by arbitration clauses drafted by the parties with the bargaining power. The reader need not strain to see that same concern for the employees in *Prudential*.

Unless and until Congress or the Supreme Court provides guidance, arbitration provisions in employment contracts or applications are likely to continue to be attacked in litigation. Community colleges interested in maintaining or implementing an arbitration program may wish to consider these two issues to help reduce vulnerability to attack:

1. ***Disclose the rights being waived.*** The arbitration agreement should state that it applies to the President's rights under Title VII of the 1964 Civil Rights Act, the Americans With Disabilities Act, the Age Discrimination in Employment Act, and the like, and that those acts confer a right to a trial by jury, to compensatory and punitive damages, and to the recovery of attorneys' fees if successful. A college should notify the president in writing that the agreement to arbitrate includes a waiver of the right to go to court but that the remedies available in court can be awarded by the arbitrator.

   The *Prudential* court harped on the unfairness of an agreement that did not clearly disclose to the employee what was being waived. Whether disclosure will satisfy the courts remains to be seen.

2. *Incorporate some or all of the statutory rights.* In *Graham Oil*, disclosure did not suffice. To meet this higher standard, an arbitration agreement should merely shift the forum of the dispute, without negating any rights to which the employee would be entitled in court. Thus, the arbitrator would be authorized to award the full range of remedies available to a judge and jury, such as compensatory and punitive damages and attorney's fees.

Incorporating these rights obviously negates some of the advantages employers may have come to expect in arbitration. But if *Graham Oil* is any indication, those advantages may be a thing of the past. The remaining advantages of arbitration— avoiding a jury and reducing the time and expense of pre-trial and trial—are still considerable.

For now, judicial scrutiny is going to require employers to weigh carefully the advantages they seek to retain in arbitration versus the risks posed by retaining those advantages. The more arbitration agreements take from employees, the more vulnerable these agreements will be to attack.

There is no one right answer applicable to all employers. Each community college should consider its own history of employment litigation and make an individualized assessment with competent and experienced legal counsel of how these risks and benefits should be balanced to serve the college's best interests.

> ◗ Preliminary results of this survey were presented at the 1995 ACCT Convention in Seattle and the 1996 AACC Convention in Atlanta.

AN OVERVIEW

THE ART

AND SCIENCE

OF

OBTAINING

RELEASES

FROM

DEPARTING

EMPLOYEES

Almost every time an employee is involuntarily terminated, the employer faces the possibility of having to defend or settle what is likely to be an expensive lawsuit or discrimination claim. As a result, colleges often use separation agreements that contain releases as a means of avoiding later wrongful discharge and discrimination claims. These releases, if properly drafted and implemented, can be an effective method of barring future suits. However, areas of uncertainty remain, and colleges need to keep abreast of the changing law. This section will highlight the most significant developments. Table 6 provides a checklist for obtaining a release.

The most important activity with regard to employee releases has taken place in the courts. Two recent decisions have focused on the application of releases to claims arising under the Age Discrimination in Employment Act (ADEA). In the first case, *DiBiase v. SmithKline Beecham Corp.*, the Third Circuit considered whether an employer must offer additional consideration to workers over forty who, as part of a general release, waive claims arising under the ADEA. In the second case, *E.E.O.C. v. Sears, Roebuck and Co.*, the Court decided if a violation of the technical waiver requirements contained in the Older Workers Benefit Protection Act (OWBPA) constitutes an independent cause of action under the ADEA.

In addition, in a surprising development, the Supreme Court declined to resolve a split in the federal courts as to whether a plaintiff must, prior to challenging the validity of a release, return benefits received as compensation for the waiver of age

TABLE 6

✔ CHECKLIST FOR OBTAINING A RELEASE

WHEN TO SEEK A RELEASE:

- Routinely?
- Problematic terminations only?
- Mass layoff/restructuring only?
- Issues to consider
- Cost estimate
- Sending the employee to a lawyer
- Taxability
- Timing of the procedure
- Consistency

WHAT THE RELEASE SHOULD COVER:

- Release of all claims (civil rights, statutory, and common law claims)
- Confidentiality
- Tax issues
- Known and unknown claims (e.g., California Civil Code Section 1542)
- Older Workers' Benefit Protection Act
- Savings clause

APPROACH:

After making the decision to terminate the employee:

- Assume the employee will seek legal counsel if you mention a release
- Assess whether mentioning a release is worth the risk
- Bring the employee into the meeting and briefly discuss the reasons for the termination
- Discuss the benefits the company will provide without a release
- Discuss additional compensation provided in exchange for a release
- Take a business-like approach; calm, matter-of-fact
- Have the release ready to give to the employee

discrimination claims. The circuit court decisions in *Oberg v. Allied Van Lines, Inc.* and *Wamsley v. Champlin Refining and Chemicals, Inc.* represent the differing views on this issue. Finally, the Seventh Circuit's decision in *Fleming v. U.S. Postal Service* is summarized as an overview of the common law "tender back" rule and its exceptions.

ANALYSIS OF RECENT COURT DECISIONS

DiBiase v. SmithKline Beecham Corp.,
48 F.3d. 719 (3rd. Cir. 1995)

In 1990, SmithKline Beecham Corporation, a pharmaceutical company based in Philadelphia, consolidated its computer operations into a single center at King of Prussia, Pennsylvania. Prior to this consolidation, SmithKline employed John DiBiase as a computer operations shift supervisor at its facility in Philadelphia. DiBiase relocated to King of Prussia but was subsequently laid off as part of a division-wide reduction in force. As compensation, SmithKline offered terminated employees a separation benefit plan that included 12 months' salary and 3 months' extended benefits. Additionally, SmithKline offered an enhanced separation plan to employees who agreed to sign a general release of all claims against SmithKline, including claims arising under the ADEA and other federal anti-discrimination statutes. DiBiase was 51 years old at the time he was terminated.

DiBiase declined to sign the release, contending the policy discriminated against older workers by requiring them to give up their rights under the ADEA. Because DiBiase did not sign the release, SmithKline refused to pay him enhanced benefits and, in June of 1993, DiBiase filed a two count complaint in the United States District Court for the Eastern District of Pennsylvania. In the first count, DiBiase alleged that SmithKline terminated him because of his age and therefore violated the ADEA. In the second count he alleged the separation plan itself violated the ADEA because it did not give additional compensation to older workers for the waiver of their ADEA claims.

In March of 1994, the district court held that, although DiBiase had not been fired due to his age, the separation plan itself violated the ADEA. Specifically, the court held that SmithKline's enhanced separation plan involved discriminatory treatment of employees protected by the ADEA.

On appeal, the Third Circuit rejected the ruling of the district court and held that SmithKline's separation policy did not discriminate against older workers. In reaching its decision, the Court noted that SmithKline's enhanced benefit plan did not mention age and that it treated all terminated employees similarly by requiring them to give up all claims. Although the release specifically included the ADEA, as well as other federal statutes, this, by itself, was held not to constitute a *per se* violation of the ADEA. The Court concluded that the existence of additional rights for older workers under the ADEA does not mean that a separation plan that requires those workers to give up such claims without additional compensation is automatically discriminatory. Therefore, the Court held that to constitute a violation, the employee's age must actually play a role in the decision-making process.

The Court of Appeals then examined whether SmithKline's separation plan discriminated against older workers on the basis of a disparate impact theory. In this type of analysis, the plaintiff claims the challenged practice has a disproportionate effect on older workers and, therefore, violates the ADEA. Normally, disparate impact claims involve a statistical comparison of the protected and unprotected classes. Although DiBiase did not present this type of evidence, the Court observed that his claim, by necessity, involved a disparate impact to all older workers. In reaching its decision to reject DiBiase's claim, the Court found guidance in a Supreme Court ruling that had held, in the context of Title VII and gender discrimination, that "[e]ven a completely neutral practice will inevitably have some disproportionate impact on one group or another" (quoting *Los Angeles Dep't of Water & Power v. Manhart*, 435 U.S. 702, 710 n. 20 (1978)). Persuaded by this reasoning, the Court concluded "it is doubtful that traditional disparate impact theory is a viable theory of liability under the ADEA."

E.E.O.C. v. Sears, Roebuck and Co.,
883 F.Supp. 211 (D. Ill. 1995)

In 1992, Sears, Roebuck and Company restructured its compensation agreement for employees selling big ticket sales items such as refrigerators and other large appliances. This arrangement was expected to decrease the pay of some employees and Sears anticipated that a few would rather resign than continue employment under the new agreement. *Id.* at 213. Sears offered all employees in this category the opportunity to participate in its "Big Ticket Severance Allowance Plan." Under this plan, employees were given five days to decide whether to remain on the job or resign and receive up to 26 weeks of severance pay. Additionally, employees who chose to resign were given 45 days to consider the option of signing a waiver of all claims in exchange for additional separation benefits.

The Equal Employment Opportunity Commission ("EEOC") brought suit claiming Sears' separation plan violated the ADEA. In its claim, the EEOC asserted that Sears did not comply with the waiver provisions of the OWBPA. Section 626(f) of the OWBPA sets forth specific provisions that must be included in all waivers for them to be considered knowing and voluntary. The EEOC contended that Sears' failure to comply with these provisions constituted a *per se* violation of the ADEA.

The District Court for the Northern District of Illinois disagreed with this reasoning and held that a violation of the OWBPA does not create a separate cause of action under the ADEA. The Court explained that, because Congress could have created a separate cause of action but chose not to, the Court was now precluded from reading such an expansive interpretation into the statute. However, the Court noted that a release that is not executed knowingly and voluntarily is nevertheless invalid under the OWBPA.

Oberg v. Allied Van Lines, Inc.,
11 F.3d 679 (7th Cir. 1993), *cert. denied*, 114 S.Ct. 2104 (1994)

As part of a reduction in its workforce, Allied Van Lines fired over sixty people, including long time employees Gerald Oberg, Nicholas Tautz, and Stephen Adams. As compensation, Allied offered all terminated employees a severance package that included two weeks of pay and benefits. Allied also offered an enhanced severance package that provided 26 weeks of pay and continued benefits in exchange for a release of all claims, including those arising under the ADEA. The release form specifically stated that if a former employee breached the agreement, that person would be required to return all severance benefits. Oberg, Tautz, and Adams each signed the release and received compensation under the enhanced plan.

After each of the three had received their last severance payments, they filed a class action complaint alleging that Allied had violated the ADEA and that the severance agreements were invalid. In their suit, the plaintiffs stipulated that they had not returned their severance benefits. Allied, in turn, admitted that the separation agreement had failed to include the waiver provisions required by the OWBPA. However, Allied contended that even if the severance agreements were initially invalid, the plaintiffs had ratified them by continuing to accept Allied's enhanced severance payments. Allied also argued, in the alternative, that the plaintiffs should have been required to tender back the severance payments as a prerequisite to filing suit under the ADEA. Finally, Allied counter-sued for damages on a breach of contract theory.

On appeal, the Seventh Circuit affirmed the lower court's decision and held the plaintiffs did not have to tender back the release money prior to bringing suit under the ADEA. The Court reasoned that the enactment of the OWBPA specifically limited the manner in which an employee could waive claims under the ADEA. Since Allied admitted that it did not include the required OWBPA waiver provisions, the Court held the severance agreements were void and unenforceable against the plaintiffs. Following this reasoning, the Court also rejected Allied's argument that the plaintiffs had ratified the agreements by continuing to accept separation benefits. Specifically, the Court held it was legally impossible for an invalid waiver to ever become ratified.

In their ruling that the plaintiffs were not required to tender back their severance benefits as a prerequisite to filing a claim under the ADEA, the Court of Appeals followed the Eleventh Circuit, which has held that the requirement to tender back severance benefits is preempted by federal law and not required under the ADEA. Finally, the Court found that, although Allied would be entitled to offset any award of damages by the amount of separation benefits already paid, Allied's breach of contract claim failed "because an unenforceable contract cannot be enforced."

Wamsley v. Champlin Refining and Chemicals, Inc.,
11 F.3d 534 (5th Cir. 1993), rehr'g en banc denied, 37 F.3d 634 (1994), cert. denied, 115 S.Ct. 1403 (1995)

In 1990, Champlin Refining and Chemicals became the wholly owned subsidiary of Citgo Petroleum Corporation. As a result of this restructuring, Champlin closed its Irving, Texas, office and several of its employees lost their jobs. Champlin offered severance benefits to those terminated employees who were willing to sign a release of all claims, including those arising under the ADEA. The release clearly stated that any severance benefits received by the employee would be compensation for the promise to give up all claims relating to their employment.

Allen Wamsley and several other terminated employees executed the releases and subsequently received severance benefits. Notwithstanding these releases, Wamsley and the other former employees filed suit in January of 1992, alleging that Champlin had made the decision to fire them on the basis of age and, therefore, violated the ADEA. Additionally, the plaintiffs alleged the releases were invalid because they had failed to comply with one of the provisions of the OWBPA. Specifically, they contended that "Champlin had failed to provide them 45 days to consider the release as required under the OWBPA, and thus, the releases were not 'knowing and voluntary' within the meaning of the section 626(f)(1) of the ADEA."

In August of 1992, the district court held the releases were valid and that the plaintiffs had waived their rights knowingly and voluntarily within the meaning of the ADEA. Furthermore, the court held that, even if the releases had not been executed knowingly and voluntarily, the plaintiffs had ratified them by failing to return their benefits after learning that the releases were allegedly invalid. On appeal, the plaintiffs first argued that the waivers had not been voluntary. Second, the plaintiff's argued that the doctrine of ratification has no application to a suit arising under the ADEA.

The Fifth Circuit agreed with the district court and held that the plaintiffs had ratified the agreement by accepting the enhanced severance payments. Although the Court acknowledged that void promises are not binding and can never be ratified, it interpreted the language of section 626(f)(1) to mean that a waiver that is not made knowingly and voluntarily is subject to being voided at the election of the employee. In essence, a defective waiver is voidable but not void. Therefore, the Court found that when the Plaintiffs "chose to retain and not tender back to Champlin the benefits paid them in consideration for their promise not to sue Champlin, they manifested their intention to be bound by the waivers and thus, made a new promise to abide by their terms."

Fleming v. U.S. Postal Service AMF O'Hare, 27 F.3d 259 (7th Cir. 1994)

Beatrice Fleming, an African-American woman who suffers from schizophrenia and hearing impairment, was fired from the U.S. Postal Service in 1986. She filed suit claiming breach of contract, retaliatory discharge, and discrimination on the basis of race, sex, and handicap. The U.S. Postal Service offered Fleming a total of $75,000 in exchange for a release of her claims, which she accepted. Several weeks later, she filed a handwritten motion to the district court claiming "that she had been 'confused, disoriented, and under a lot of pressure'" when she agreed to the release. The district court judge denied the motion without comment and Fleming appealed.

The Seventh Circuit refused to overturn the district court's order and held that Fleming's claim was barred by her failure to tender back her settlement payment. Although the "principle that a release can be rescinded only upon a tender of any consideration received is . . . a general principle of contract law," Judge Posner noted that "the common law rule requiring tender as a prerequisite to recision may have to give way" when federal law limits a class of releases. Examples of federal laws that may, in some circumstances, preempt this common law doctrine, include the Federal Employers' Liability Act, the Jones Act, and the Age Discrimination in Employment Act. *Id.* at 261; *e.g., Oberg v. Allied*

Van Lines, Inc., supra (holding that ADEA preempts the common law tender back rule).

The Court then reviewed several other exceptions to the tender back rule. For example, the requirement is waived when a plaintiff is unable to secure the funds necessary to pay the defendant. Additionally, the Court found it not problematic to waive the requirement in "the case in which all the plaintiff obtained in exchange for the release was something to which he was already entitled." Although the Ninth Circuit has held that a plaintiff is not required to return release money as a prerequisite to bringing a claim under 42 U.S.C. § 1983, the Seventh Circuit noted that it was not willing to add this statute to the list of exceptions. *Id.; see Botefur v. City of Eagle Point*, 7 F.3d 152, 155-156 (9th Cir. 1993). In refusing to grant Fleming's motion, the Court noted that, although there are valid exceptions to the common law tender back rule, the list is not endless. As Judge Posner stated, "[n]ot even plaintiffs are helped in the long run by a rule allowing them to have their cake and eat it, for a defendant will not pay as much for a release that the plaintiff can challenge without having to repay the money as the price of maintaining the challenge."

To assist CEOs and trustees in making informed decisions about separation prior to employment, Sample III offers an example of a separation and general release document.

Stephen J. Hirschfeld, a partner with McKenna & Cuneo, L.L.P., in San Francisco, specializes in labor, employment, and higher education law.

COMMUNITY COLLEGE CEO EMPLOYMENT AGREEMENT

PRESIDENT'S EMPLOYMENT CONTRACT

This Agreement is made between the Board of Trustees of *[Full legal name and address of Institution]* ("Board"), and *[Full name and address of Other Contracting Party]* ("President").

1.0 Appointment as President.

1.1 Board appoints and employs [name of President] to be president of the Institution, to serve as the chief executive officer of the Institution under policies, supervision, and direction of Board and its Executive Committee. President accepts and agrees to such employment.

1.2 President shall perform all duties required by law, by the Agreement, and by custom and practice to be performed by a college president including, but not limited to:

1.2.1 Fund raising, development, public and alumni relations;

1.2.2 Institutional, faculty, and educational leadership;

1.2.3 Long-range planning; budget formulation; supervision of Institution buildings, grounds, and equipment controlled by this Institution; administration of the affairs of the Institution as best serves the Institution consistent with Board policy;

1.2.4 Student recruitment and services; faculty recruitment;

1.2.5 Appointing, supervising, promoting, and dismissing staff members;

1.2.6 Preparing regulations, rules, and procedures useful for the welfare of the Institution.

2.0 Devote Best Efforts to the Work as President.

2.1 President agrees to devote, faithfully, industriously, and with maximum application of experience, ability, and talent, full time, attention, and energies to the duties as President of the Institution.

2.2 Such duties shall be rendered at the campus of the Institution in *[City]*, *[State]*, and at such other place or places as Board or President shall deem appropriate for the interest, needs, business, or opportunity of the Institution.

2.3 The expenditure of reasonable amounts of time for personal or outside business, as well as charitable and professional development activities, shall not be deemed a breach of this Agreement, provided such activities do not interfere with the services required to be rendered to Board under the provisions of this Agreement.

2.4 President shall not, without prior written permission from the Board, render services of any professional nature to or for any person or firm for remuneration other than to Board, and shall absolutely not engage in any activity that may be competitive with and adverse to the best interest of Board. The making of passive and personal investments and the conduct of private business affairs shall not be prohibited hereunder.

3.0 *Term of Appointment; Evaluation; Renewal.*

3.1 This appointment shall be for a term of _____ years, commencing _____, and terminating _____, subject, however, to prior termination as provided for in this Agreement.

3.2 After the completion of approximately _____ months of the term of this agreement, and annually thereafter, a committee of Board shall meet with President to evaluate and discuss President's performance. To aid Board in such annual job performance reviews, President agrees to furnish such oral and written reports as may be required by Board.

3.3 Board, in its sole discretion, may offer to extend this Agreement for _____ additional years upon the terms and conditions contained in this Agreement or upon such additional or different terms as may be agreed upon by President and Board.

4.0 *Salary.*

4.1 For all services rendered under this Agreement, Board shall pay President an annual salary of _____ dollars ($_____), payable in equal *monthly* installments. Salary shall include deductions for local, state, and federal taxes and employee benefits.

4.2 President's salary shall be reviewed annually and may be increased but not decreased at the discretion of Board. Such annual salary review will be in conjunction with a review by Board or a Board committee of the performance of President.

4.3 President shall be responsible for any income tax liability incurred as a result of this Agreement.

5.0 *Insurance and Retirement Benefits.*

5.1 Board shall provide President with health care coverage [describe coverage or attach and incorporate by reference a separate description], and disability insurance in the amount of _____ dollars ($_____).

5.2 Board will maintain for President term life insurance coverage in an amount as determined by Board from time to time, but not less than _____ dollars ($_____).

5.3 President shall be an employee of Board for the purposes of being covered by Board's Workers' Compensation policy.

5.4 President shall be entitled to participate in the _____ College Retirement Program to which Board shall contribute _____ dollars ($_____) annually.

6.0 *Sick Leave.*

President shall be allowed _____ days of sick leave per year, which may be accumulated.

7.0 *Housing.*

7.1 As a condition of employment, President agrees to live in, and Board agrees to provide, maintain in good repair, and pay for utilities and telephone service for a residence located at [insert address]. Board shall provide for maintenance of the grounds on which the residence is situated.

7.1.1 The residence shall be furnished with furniture and furnishings at the cost of the [Board/President]. Board shall keep said residence property insured for fire and extended coverage and shall pay for liability insurance on said property. The cost of any insurance on the contents of said residence shall be borne by the [Board/President].

[alternative]

[7.1 Board shall provide President an allowance of _____ dollars ($_____) annually, paid in equal monthly installments, to purchase or lease housing.]

8.0 *Automobile.*

    8.1   As a condition of employment, Board shall furnish President with an automobile *[to be used exclusively for Institution business]*. This vehicle shall be maintained by Board, and all fuel for the use thereof shall be paid by Board.

    8.2   Said vehicle shall be insured at the cost of Board with limits of $_____ per individual and $_____ per accident, and President shall be a named insured.

9.0 *Professional Dues and Meetings.*

Board will provide _____ dollars ($_____) per year for reasonable expenses incurred by President to attend educational conferences, conventions, courses seminars and other similar professional growth activities, including membership in professional organizations.

10.0 *Travel for the Institution.*

Board will provide _____ dollars ($_____) per year for President and President's spouse's reasonable travel expenses, hotel bills, and other necessary and proper expenses when President is traveling on Institution business, except that payments will be made on behalf of the spouse only when the presence of the spouse is necessary to further the interests of the Institution.

11.0 *Entertainment Allowance.*

Board will provide _____ dollars ($_____) per year for reasonable expenses incurred by President for Institution-related entertaining.

12.0 *Membership in Service Organizations.*

Board will provide President with membership in *[insert number]* clubs or service organizations that would further the interests of the Institution.

13.0 *Expense Receipts and Documentation.*

President agrees to maintain and furnish an accounting of expenses provided for in this Agreement in reasonable detail on a quarterly basis.

14.0 *Tenure.*

[Insert name of President] [waives any right to academic tenure at the Institution/is granted tenure in the Department of _____/retains previously granted tenure in this Institution's Department of _____.]

15.0 *Vacations and Personal Leave.*

15.1 President shall be entitled annually to _____ working days of paid vacation. Attendance at business and professional meetings and conferences shall not be construed as vacation time. Unless otherwise agreed, such vacation shall not accumulate from year to year.

15.2 Board shall give President _____ working days of personal leave with pay during each year of the term of this Agreement. Unless otherwise agreed, personal leave time will not accumulate from year to year. At the expiration of the term of this Agreement, President will be entitled to payment for unused vacation and personal leave time.

15.3 President shall not take vacation, personal, or professional leave if such leave interferes with properly discharging the duties under the terms of this Agreement.

16.0 *Working Facilities.*

President will be furnished with a private office, secretarial assistance and such other facilities and services suitable to the position and adequate for the performance of the duties.

17.0 *Termination and Liquidated Damages.*

17.1 *Termination by Institution for Just Cause.* The parties agree that the Institution may terminate this Agreement at any time for "just cause," which, in addition to any of its other normally understood meanings in employment contracts, shall include the following:

17.1.1 A deliberate or serious violation of the duties set forth in this Agreement or refusal or unwillingness to perform such duties in good faith and to the best of President's abilities;

17.1.2 A violation by President of any of the other terms and conditions of this Agreement not remedied after *thirty* (30) days' written notice thereof to President;

17.1.3 Any conduct of President that constitutes moral turpitude, or that would tend to bring public disrespect, contempt, or ridicule upon the Institution;

17.1.4 A deliberate or serious violation of any law, rule, regulation, Constitutional provision or bylaw of the Institution, or local, state, or federal law, which violation may, in the sole judgment of Board, reflect adversely upon the Institution;

17.1.5 Prolonged absence from duty without the Institution's consent.

17.2 *Termination by Institution Without Cause.* The parties agree that the Institution may terminate this Agreement prior to its normal expiration, without cause, which, in addition to any of its other normally understood meanings in employment contracts, shall include the following situations:

17.2.1 Regardless of any other provision of this Agreement, this Agreement shall terminate automatically if President dies or becomes totally disabled, or totally incapacitated or incapable of carrying out the duties as President, as defined by the Institution.

17.2.1.1 If Board deems President disabled, totally incapacitated, or incapable of carrying out the duties as President, Board reserves the right to require President to submit to a medical examination, either physical or mental. Such examination shall be performed by a physician licensed to practice medicine in all of its branches, selected and paid for by Board.

17.2.1.2 If President becomes incapable of carrying out the duties of office, due to permanent disability or incapacity and is terminated, Board shall be liable to President or President's personal representative, as the case may be, for any accrued but unpaid compensation together with a proportionate part of any other benefits which would be due and payable to President, or personal representative, as the case may be, by reason of death or incapacity during employment by Board.

17.2.1.3 President shall receive a monthly salary payment for _____ months, which may be a combination of long-term disability insurance payments and wages, if permitted by the terms of the insurance policy, or be comprised totally of wages paid by the Institution.

[alternate 17.2.1.3]:

[17.2.1.3 No payments shall be provided if President becomes disabled and is terminated.]

17.2.2 This Agreement may be terminated at any time by the Institution by delivering to President written notice of the Institution's intent to terminate this Agreement without cause, which notice shall be effective *[thirty]* (30) days after the date the notice is delivered. In such event, President shall be entitled to damages only as provided for in the liquidated damages clause set forth below.

17.3 *Liquidated Damages.* If Institution terminates this Agreement without cause under section 17.2.2 above, Institution shall pay President, as liquidated damages, an amount equal to _____% of President's base annual salary.

17.3.1 Institution shall pay its obligation on a monthly basis prorated over the balance of the term of this Agreement and shall be subject to President's duty to mitigate as set forth below. President will be entitled to continue the health insurance plan and group life insurance at President's expense for up to eighteen[1] months from the effective date of termination but will not be entitled to any other benefits except as otherwise provided or required by applicable law. In no case shall the Institution be liable for the loss of any collateral business opportunities or any other benefits, perquisites, or

[1]*Editor's Note: This is what is allowed under federal law. Users of this form should research their own state laws regarding this issue, as some states may have created a longer entitlement period.*

income from any sources that may ensue as a result of the Institution's termination of the Agreement without cause.

17.3.2 The parties have bargained for and agreed to the foregoing liquidated damages provision, giving consideration to the fact that termination of this Agreement by the Institution without cause prior to its natural expiration may cause loss to President which damages are extremely difficult to determine with certainty. The parties further agree that the payment of such liquidated damages by the Institution and acceptance thereof by President shall constitute adequate and reasonable compensation to President for the damages and injury suffered.

17.4 *Mitigation of Damages.* Regardless of the damages provisions, President agrees to mitigate the Institution's obligations to pay liquidated damages under this Agreement, and to make reasonable and diligent efforts to obtain employment. After President obtains such new employment, the Institution's financial obligations under this Agreement, including liquidated damages, shall cease.

17.5 *Termination by President.* This Agreement may be terminated without cause by President giving the Institution *thirty (30)* days' advance written notice of the termination of employment with the Institution, [except that President shall not have the right to terminate this Agreement during the _____-month period prior to the expiration of this Agreement.]

17.5.1 If President exercises the right under this provision to terminate this Agreement, the Institution shall be entitled to _____% of President's base annual salary.

17.5.2 The parties have bargained for and agreed to the foregoing liquidated damages provision, giving consideration to the fact that termination of this Agreement by the President without cause prior to its natural expiration may cause loss to Institution, which damages are extremely difficult to determine with certainty. The parties further agree that the payment of such liquidated damages by the Institution and acceptance thereof by President shall constitute adequate and reasonable compensation to President for the damages and injury suffered.

17.5.3 If President so terminates this Agreement, President agrees that at the sole discretion and option of Board, President shall continue to work for the ensuing _____-month period at the same salary and with the same normal benefits, provided, however, that Board would not be liable to President for any accrued vacation or personal leave time.

17.5.4 In no case shall the Institution by liable for the loss of any benefits, perquisites, or income from any other sources.

18.0 *Entire Agreement; Modification.*

This agreement constitutes the entire understanding of the parties hereto and supersedes any and all prior or contemporaneous representations or agreements, whether written or oral, between the parties, and cannot be changed or modified unless in writing signed by the parties hereto.

19.0 *Severability.*

The terms of this Agreement are severable such that if any term or provision is declared by a court of competent jurisdiction to be illegal, void, or unenforceable, the remainder of the provisions shall continue to be valid and enforceable.

20.0 *Governing Law; Forum.*

This Agreement shall be interpreted and construed in accordance with the laws of the State of _____, which shall be the forum for any lawsuit arising from or incident to this Agreement.

21.0 *Waiver.*

No delay or failure to enforce any provision of this Agreement shall constitute a waiver or limitation of rights enforceable under this Agreement.

22.0 *Non-Assignable.*

This Agreement is not assignable but shall be binding upon the heirs, administrators, personal representatives, successors, and assigns of both parties.

23.0 *Time Is of the Essence of This Agreement.*

Time is of the essence of this Agreement.

IN WITNESS WHEREOF, *[Name of President]* and the authorized representative(s) of Institution have executed this Agreement on this _____ day of _____, 19___.

INSTITUTION:

[Full Legal Name of Institution]

by_____
(Signature, Chair of the Governing Board)

_____
(Printed Name)

_____
(Title)

PRESIDENT:

[Full Legal Name of Contracting Party]

by _____
(Signature)

_____
(Printed Name)

_____
(Title)

EXECUTIVE EMPLOYMENT AGREEMENT

SAMPLE II

E MPLOYMENT AGREEMENT (the "Agreement") dated as of September ___, 1996 by and between XYZ COMPANY, a California corporation (the "Employer"), and JOHN/JANE DOE, a resident of the State of Arizona (the "Employee").

WHEREAS, the Employer provides consulting services throughout the United States; and

WHEREAS, the Employee has represented to the Employer he/she has considerable knowledge and experience in the consulting business and could significantly grow and expand the businesses of the Employer; and

WHEREAS, the Employer has indicated to the Employee that it is the Employer's objective to increase substantially its business, including the addition of more space and equipment; and

WHEREAS, the parties understand that the Employer's interest in growth and expansion is important to the Employee and is an important consideration in his/her decision to accept an offer of employment with the Employer; and

WHEREAS, the Employee has assured the Employer that he/she can develop substantial new business for the Employer, and the parties acknowledge that such ability to attract new business is a key factor in the willingness of the Employer to offer employment to the Employee hereunder; and

WHEREAS, the Employer understands that to add substantive new sales will require additional investment in people, facilities, and state of the art equipment to support new markets; and

WHEREAS, based on the foregoing and other considerations, the Employer desires to employ the Employee as its President, and the Employee desires to be so employed, upon the terms and conditions hereinafter set forth;

NOW, THEREFORE, the parties hereto, intending to be legally bound, hereby agree as follows:

1.0 **Employment.** The Employer hereby employs the Employee, and the Employee hereby accepts such employment and agrees to perform the duties and responsibilities hereunder, in accordance with the terms and conditions hereinafter set forth.

    1.1 **Employment Term.** The employment term of this Agreement (the "Employment Term") shall commence on October 1, 1996 and shall continue until and expire on September 30, 1998, unless terminated earlier in accordance with Section 8 hereof or extended by mutual written agreement of the Employer and the Employee.

    1.2 **Duties and Responsibilities.**

        (a) During the Employment Term, the Employee shall serve as the President of the Employer and shall perform all duties and accept all responsibilities incidental to such position or as may be assigned to him/her by the Employer's Board of Directors (the "Employer's Board") or its Chairperson, and he/she shall cooperate fully with the Employer's Board and its Chairperson.

        (b) As President of the Employer, the Employee shall have general supervision over and control of the Employer's normal operations and activities, subject in all cases to the supervision and control of the Employer's Board and its Chairperson. In such capacity, the Employee shall have access to all regularly prepared financial statements, which he/she agrees to safeguard as if they were his/her own confidential information, and he/she shall have the power and authority necessary to carry out his/her duties and responsibilities as chief operating officer, including without limitation the power and authority to (i) make employment decisions and negotiate collective bargaining agreements with labor unions; (ii) sign checks in the ordinary course of business consistent with applicable corporate policies; (iii) enter into agreements, contracts, leases and commitments in the ordinary course of business provided that they are consistent with approved budgets, but not notes, loan agreements or other agreements relating to the borrowing or investment of money or the mortgaging or granting of any security interest in assets unless otherwise authorized by the Board of Directors or Chairperson; and (iv) take all other actions as may be necessary or appropriate to carry on the normal business of the Employer, consistent with all applicable bylaws and with any instructions or directions of the Employer's Board or its Chairperson.

(c)   The Employee represents to the Employer that he/she is not currently subject or a party to, and agrees that he/she will not after the date hereof become subject or a party to, any employment agreement, non-competition covenant, non-disclosure agreement or other agreement, covenant, understanding or restriction that would prohibit the Employee from executing this Agreement or performing fully the duties and responsibilities hereunder, or which would in any manner, directly or indirectly, limit or affect the duties and responsibilities that may now or in the future be assigned to the Employee by the Employer. The Employee further represents that he/she has had a recent medical examination and believes that he/she is in good overall health and able to perform the essential elements of the job hereunder.

1.3   *Extent of Service.* During the Employment Term, the Employee shall use his/her best efforts in the business of the Employer, and shall devote substantially his/her full time, attention and energy to the business of the Employer and to the performance of his/her services and the discharge of his/her duties and responsibilities hereunder. Except as provided in Section 5.1 hereof, the foregoing shall not be construed as preventing the Employee from making investments in other businesses or enterprises provided that the Employee agrees not to become engaged in any other business activity that may interfere with his/her ability to discharge the duties and responsibilities hereunder to the Employer. The Employee further agrees not to work on either a part time or independent contractual basis for any other business or enterprise during the Employment Term without the prior written approval of the Employer's Board or its Chairperson.

1.4 *Base Compensation.*

(a) For all the services rendered and to be rendered by the Employee hereunder, the Employer shall pay the Employee an annual salary at the rate of $_____, less such withholding and other deductions as may be required by law or any employee benefit plan in which the Employee participates, payable in installments at such times as the Employer customarily pays its executive officers.

(b) During the Employment Term, the Employee also shall be (i) entitled to _____ weeks of paid vacation and _____ days of paid sick leave in each calendar year of the Employment Term (prorated for that part of the Employment Term ending on December 31, 1996), (ii) provided the use of a new automobile and reimbursement of all reasonable expenses related thereto (but only one automobile for the Employment Term), and (iii) permitted to participate in such life insurance, disability, medical and other fringe benefit programs of the Employer as may exist from time to time on the same basis as other senior executives.

1.5 *Incentive Compensation.* In addition to the base compensation described in Section 1.4(a) above, for each calendar year of the Employment Term the Employee shall be entitled to a performance bonus equal to the sum of (i) .05% of the pre-tax adjusted operating income of the Employer before the payment of any other bonuses to executives, otherwise in accordance with generally accepted accounting principles, plus (ii) 1% of the total net selling price actually received by the Employer during each year of this Agreement from sales to accounts personally developed by the Employee and with respect to which no sales commissions or other similar payments are payable to other persons. The Employee shall maintain and provide to the Chairperson of the Employer on a regular basis a list of those accounts that he/she believes meet the standard set forth in the immediately preceding sentence, which list shall be for informational purposes only and not binding upon the Employer. The performance bonus referred to in clauses (i) and (ii) above, if any, shall be paid within 30 days after the delivery to the Employer of an audited, annual combined income statement of the Employer prepared by the Employer's outside accounting and auditing firm on the above basis, which statement shall be binding on the Employer and the Employee for purposes of determining that portion of any performance bonus payable by the Employer to the Employee under clause (i) above for the year in question and not subject to any challenge or appeal by either party. For the calendar year 1996, that part of the performance bonus payable under clause (i) above shall be determined by taking the amount as calculated for 1996 and multiplying such amount by a fraction, the numerator of which shall be the number of days included in the Employment Term for 1996 and the denominator of which shall be 366.

2.0 *Expense Reimbursement.*

2.1 *Moving.* The Employer will reimburse the Employee for the reasonable expenses incurred by the Employee in moving from his/her current residence in Phoenix, Arizona to the San Francisco, California area upon presentation to the Employer of an itemized account and written proof of such expenses, and it also will reimburse him/her for any future relocation expenses should the Employee move again at the request of the Employer. The Employee will obtain three separate quotes for moving expenses from reputable moving companies and will use the company providing the lowest quote unless the acceptance of a higher quote is approved in advance by the Employer's Chairperson. Air fare at coach rates shall be included for not more than two trips per month, and the move to San Francisco will be concluded within six months.

2.2 *Business.* The Employer also will reimburse the Employee for all ordinary and necessary out-of-pocket business expenses incurred in connection with the discharge of his/her duties and responsibilities hereunder during the Employment Term in accordance with the Employer's expense approval procedures then in effect and upon presentation to the Employer of an itemized account and written proof of such expenses. Extraordinary expenses, such as country club memberships, shall be subject to the prior approval of the Employer's Chairperson.

3.0 **Developments.** The Employee shall disclose fully, promptly and in writing to the Employer any and all inventions, discoveries, improvements, modifications and the like, whether patentable or not, which he/she conceives, makes or develops, solely or jointly with others, while employed by the Employer and that (i) relate to the business, work or activities of the Employer or (ii) result from or are suggested by the carrying out of his/her duties hereunder, or from or by any information which he/she may receive while employed by the Employer. The Employee hereby assigns, transfers and conveys to the Employer or its designee all of his/her right, title and interest in and to any and all such inventions, discoveries, improvements, modifications and the like and agrees to take all such actions as may be requested by the Employer at any time and with respect to any such invention, discovery, improvement, modification or the like to confirm or evidence such assignment, transfer and conveyance.

4.0 **Confidential Information.** The Employee acknowledges that, by reason of his/her employment with the Employer, he/she will have access to confidential, financial and other proprietary information of and about the Employer (collectively, "Confidential Information"). The Employee acknowledges that such Confidential Information is a valuable and unique asset of the Employer and covenants that, both during and after the Employment Term, he/she will not disclose any Confidential Information to any person or discuss the business of the Employer with any person (except in any case as his/her duties as the President of the Employer may require) without the prior written authorization of the Employer's Board or its Chairperson. The obligation of confidentiality imposed by this Section 4.0 shall not apply to information that appears in issued patents or printed publications, which otherwise becomes generally known in the industry through no act of the Employee in breach of this Agreement or that is required to be disclosed by court order or applicable law.

5.0 **Non-Competition; No Solicitation.**

5.1 **Non-Competition.** During the stated term of the Employment Term and without regard to its early termination for any reason under either Section 8.4 or 8.5 hereof, the Employee shall not, pursuant hereto or with the prior written consent of the Employer's Board or its Chairperson, directly or indirectly, own, manage, operate, finance, join, control or participate in the ownership, management, operation, financing or control of, or be connected as an officer, director, employee, partner, principal, agent, representative, consultant or otherwise with, or use or permit his/her name to be used in connection with, any business or enterprise engaged in the business of _____ within any state of the United States or the District of Columbia; *provided, however,* that notwithstanding the foregoing, (i) this provision shall not be construed to prohibit the passive ownership by the Employee of not more than 1% of the capital stock of any corporation that is engaged in the _____ business having a class of securities registered pursuant to the Securities Exchange Act of 1934. In the event that the provisions of this Section 5.1 should ever be adjudicated to exceed the time, geographic, product or other limitations permitted by applicable law in any jurisdiction, then such provisions shall be deemed reformed in such jurisdiction to the maximum time, geographic, product or other limitations permitted by applicable law.

5.2 *No Solicitation.* During the stated term of the Employment Term and without regard to its early termination for any reason under any of Sections 8.4 or 8.5 hereof, the Employee shall not, unless acting as an Employee pursuant hereto or with the prior written consent of the Employer's Board or its Chairperson, call on, or solicit, either directly or indirectly, any person, firm, corporation or other entity who or which is a customer of the Employer, nor shall he/she offer employment to or employ, either directly or indirectly, any person who is an employee of the Employer during such time, unless such person shall have left such employment by the Employer prior to both the termination of the Employment Term and the commencement of any discussions with the Employee about employment.

6.0 *Release from Restrictions.* The parties acknowledge that the Employee has agreed to the restrictions contained in Section 5.0 above insofar as they relate to the early termination of his/her employment under either Section 8.4 or 8.5 because of the Employer's obligation under such Sections to continue to make the salary payments called for by Section 1.4(a) hereof and the other payments referred to in those Sections and to be responsible for certain other liabilities and obligations to the Employee as specified therein. If the Employee is terminated without cause under Section 8.4 hereof or elects to terminate his/her employment under Section 8.5 hereof upon a change of control and in either case the Employer fails to make the payments to the Employee required under whichever of such Sections is applicable (except where such failure to pay is excused as provided in the last sentence of Section 8.4 because of the Employee's failure to comply with his/her obligations under Section 5.0 above), and such failure continues for 20 days following receipt of notice from the Employee of such failure, the Employee shall thereafter cease to be bound by any of the restrictions found in Section 5.1 hereof (but the Employer shall remain bound to make any payments required by Section 8.4 or 8.5 hereof, as applicable).

7.0　*Equitable Relief.*

　7.1　*Restrictions.*

　　(a)　The Employee acknowledges that the restrictions contained in Sections 3.0, 4.0 and 5.0 hereof are, in view of the nature of the business of the Employer, reasonable and necessary to protect the legitimate interests of the Employer, that the Employer would not have entered into this Agreement in the absence of such restrictions, that the business of the Employer is national in scope and that any violation of any provision of those Sections could result in irreparable injury to the Employer.

　　(b)　The Employee agrees that in the event of any violation of the restrictions referred to in Section 7.1(a) above, and upon proof of actual damages, the Employer shall be entitled to preliminary and permanent injunctive relief and to an equitable accounting of all earnings, profits and other benefits arising from any such violation, which rights shall be cumulative and in addition to any other rights or remedies to which the Employer may be entitled.

　　(c)　The Employee irrevocably and unconditionally agrees that in the event of any violation of the restrictions referred to in Section 7.1(a) above, an action may be commenced for preliminary and permanent injunctive relief and other equitable relief in any federal or state court of competent jurisdiction sitting in the City and

County of San Francisco, California or in any other court of competent jurisdiction. The Employee hereby waives, to the fullest extent permitted by law, any objection that he/she may now or hereafter have to such jurisdiction or to the laying of the venue of any such suit, action or proceeding brought in such a court and any claim that such suit, action or proceeding has been brought in an inconvenient forum. The Employee agrees that effective service of process may be made upon him/her by mail under the notice provisions contained in Section 10.0 hereof and that all pleadings, notices and other papers may be served upon him/her in the same manner.

(d)   The Employee agrees that he/she will provide and that the Employer may similarly provide, a copy of Sections 3.0, 4.0 and 5.0 of this Agreement to any business or enterprise (i) that he/she may directly or indirectly own, manage, operate, finance, join, control or participate in the ownership, management, operation, financing or control of, or (ii) with which he/she may be connected with as an officer, director, employee, partner, principal, agent, representative, consultant or otherwise, or in connection with which he/she may use or permit his/her name to be used; *provided, however,* that this provision shall not apply in respect of Section 5.0 of this Agreement after expiration of the time periods set forth therein.

(e)   The Employee represents and acknowledges that (i) he/she has been advised by the Employer to consult his/her own legal counsel in respect of this Agreement and (ii) he/she has, prior to the execution of this Agreement, reviewed thoroughly this Agreement with his/her counsel.

8.0   *Termination.*

8.1   *Partial or Total Disability.* If in the judgment of the Employer's Board or its Chairperson, the Employee is unable to perform his/her duties and responsibilities hereunder by reason of illness, injury or incapacity for three consecutive months, or for more than three months in the aggregate during any period of 12 calendar months, during which time the Employer shall continue to compensate the Employee hereunder (with such compensation to be reduced by the amount of any payments due the Employee for this time period under any applicable disability benefit programs, including Social Security disability, workers' compensation and disability retirement benefits), the Employment Term may be terminated by the Employer in which event the Employer shall have no further liability or obligation to the Employee except for (i) unpaid salary and benefits accrued to the date of his/her termination, (ii) any additional disability or other benefits or payments (excluding any other severance benefits or payments) otherwise payable to the Employee under any applicable formal policy or plan of the Employer that covers the Employee at the time of his/her termination and (iii) a pro rata portion of the performance bonus, if any, referred to in Section 1.5 hereof in respect of the period prior to the date on which the Employee first became disabled. The Employee agrees, in the event of any dispute under this Section 8.1 and if requested by the Employer, to submit to a physical examination by a licensed physician mutually agreed upon by the Employer and the Employee, the cost of such examination to be paid by the Employer.

8.2   **Death.** In the event that the Employee dies during the Employment Term, the Employer shall pay to his/her executors, administrators or personal representatives, as appropriate, an amount equal to the installment of his/her salary payable for the month in which he/she dies. Thereafter, the Employer shall have no further liability or obligation to the Employee's executors, administrators, personal representatives, heirs, assigns or any other person claiming under or through him/her, except for (i) any benefits or other payments (excluding any severance benefits or payments) otherwise payable to the Employee under any applicable formal policy or plan of the Employer that covered the Employee at the time of his/her death and (ii) a pro rata portion of the performance bonus, if any, referred to in Section 1.5 hereof in respect of the period prior to the date on which the Employee died.

8.3   **For Cause.** Nothing in this Agreement shall be construed to prevent the termination of the Employment Term by the Employer at any time for "cause." For purposes of this Agreement, "cause" shall mean the failure of the Employee to observe or perform (other than by reason of illness, injury or incapacity) any of the material terms or provisions of this Agreement provided that the Employee has been given written notice of such failure and such failure has continued for 30 days thereafter, dishonesty, willful misconduct, conviction of a felony or other crime involving moral turpitude, misappropriation of funds, habitual insobriety, substance abuse, any action on the part of the Employee involving willful and deliberate malfeasance or gross negligence in the performance of his/her duties and responsibilities hereunder. Thereafter, the Employer shall have no further liability or obligation to the Employee except for the payment of unpaid salary and benefits (excluding any performance bonus) accrued to the date of his/her termination. Should the Employee be terminated for cause hereunder, the Employer will provide the Employee with a written statement detailing such cause.

8.4 **Without Cause.** The Employer, by action of the Employer's Board or its Chairperson, may terminate the Employment Term at any time without cause upon 30 days' prior notice to the Employee, in which event the Employer shall be obligated (i) to continue to make the salary payments called for by Section 1.4(a) hereof for the balance of the Employment Term specified in Section 1.1 hereof, the same as if such termination of the Employment Term had not occurred, and (ii) to pay the Employee an additional $_____ per month (pro-rated for any partial month) for each remaining month thereof not to exceed, however, $_____ in the aggregate, but the Employer shall have no other liability or obligation to the Employee except for (1) any benefits or payments (excluding any other severance benefits or payments) otherwise payable to the Employee under any applicable formal policy or plan of the Employer that covers the Employee at the time of his/her termination and (2) a pro rata portion of the performance bonus, if any, referred to in Section 1.5(i) and (ii) hereof in respect of the period prior to the date of termination (calculated by taking the amount otherwise payable for the calendar year in question and multiplying it by a fraction, the numerator of which would be the number of days in such year up to but excluding the date of termination of the Employment Term and the denominator of which would be the actual number of days in the year, either 365 or 366, as appropriate).

The Employer's obligations under clauses (i) and (ii) above are subject to the Employee's compliance with his/her obligations under Section 5.0 above and, if the Employee fails to comply with such Section 5.0, the Employer shall be forever relieved of such obligations under clauses (i) and (ii) of this Section 8.4.

8.5 *Upon a Change of Control.* The Employee may terminate the Employment Term at any time within 90 days after (i) MR. SMITH ceases to be the Chairperson of the Employer's Board for any reason other than his/her death or disability, (ii) the Employer merges or consolidates with another corporation and MR. SMITH is not the Chairperson of the surviving corporation, (iii) the Employer sells or otherwise transfers substantially all of its assets to another corporation the voting stock that is not at least 50% owned, directly or indirectly, by MR. SMITH or the Employer, (iv) the Employee is directed to report to any person other than MR. SMITH (or the Employer's Board provided that MR. SMITH is the Chairperson thereof), or (v) MR. SMITH or his/her estate owns or otherwise controls less than 50% of the outstanding voting stock of the Employer. In the event of such a termination by the Employee, the Employer's obligations to the Employee shall be the same as those provided after a termination without cause under Section 8.4 above, including the last sentence of that Section. In the event of MR. SMITH's death or disability, the Employee may not exercise his/her rights hereunder until the earlier of one year from the date of MR. SMITH's death or disability or the appointment of a new Chairperson of the Employer who takes an active role in the Employer's business as its chief executive officer.

9.0 *Survival.* Notwithstanding the termination of the Employment Term for any reason whatsoever, the obligations of the Employee under Sections 3.0, 4.0 and 5.0 hereof shall survive and remain in full force and effect to the extent and for the periods therein and in Section 6.0 hereof provided, and the provisions for equitable relief found in Section 7.0 hereof shall continue in force.

10.0 *Notices.* All notices and other communications hereunder shall be in writing and deemed to have been given when hand delivered, in person or by a recognized courier or delivery service, when telexed to the recipient's correct telefax number (with receipt confirmed) or when mailed by registered or certified mail, return receipt requested, as follows (provided that notice of change of address shall be deemed given only when received):

If to the Employer, to:

XYZ COMPANY

If by mail: xxxxxxxx
xxxxxxxx, CA xxxxx

If by hand: Suite 100
xxxxxxxx
xxxxxxxx, CA xxxxx
Attention: Mr. John Smith, Chairperson

With a required copy to:

xxxxxxxxx
xxxxxxxxx
xxxxxxxxx
Attention: xxxxxxxxxxxx

If to the Employee, to:

JOHN/JANE DOE
c/o McKenna & Cuneo, L.L.P.
One Market Plaza
Steuart Street Tower, 27th Floor
San Francisco, CA 94105

or to such other name or address as any designated recipient shall specify by notice to the other designated recipients in the manner specified in this Section 10.0. Any communication delivered in another manner shall be deemed given only when actually received by the intended recipient.

11.0 *Governing Law.* This Agreement shall be governed by and interpreted under the laws of the State of California without giving effect to any conflict of laws provisions.

12.0 *Indemnification.* In serving as an officer of the Employer, the Employee shall be entitled to rely upon the rights to indemnification provided in Article VII of the Employer's By-Laws, a copy of which has been provided to the Employee. During the Employment Term, the Employer shall not make any change in this Article VII

that would materially adversely affect the Employee's rights there-
under.

13.0 *Arbitration.* Except for the ability of the Employer to seek equitable
or injunctive relief as provided in Section 7.0 hereof, and all
matters relating thereto, all other disputes between the Employer
and the Employee hereunder shall be settled by arbitration before
three arbitrators pursuant to the commercial arbitration rules of the
American Arbitration Association, in San Francisco, California;
provided, however, that any award pursuant to such arbitration
shall be accompanied by a written opinion of the arbitrators giving
the reasons for the award. The arbitrators shall be selected by the
joint agreement of the Employer and the Employee, but if they do
not so agree within 30 days of the date of request for arbitration,
the selection shall be made pursuant to the rules of such Association. The award rendered by the arbitrators shall be conclusive and
binding upon the parties hereto, and judgment upon the award may
be entered in any court having jurisdiction thereof or application
may be made to such court for a judicial acceptance of the award
and an order of enforcement. Each party shall pay its own expenses
of arbitration and the expenses of the arbitrators (including their
compensation) shall be equally shared; except that if any matter of
dispute raised by a party or any defense or objection thereto was
unreasonable, the arbitrators may assess, as part of their award, all
or any part of the arbitration expenses (including reasonable
attorneys' fees) of the other party and of the arbitrators against the
party raising such unreasonable matter of dispute or defense or
objection thereto. Nothing herein set forth shall prevent the
Employer and the Employee from settling any dispute by mutual
agreement at any time or from agreeing to have any arbitration
conducted by a single arbitrator.

14.0 *Contents of Agreement.*

14.1 *Amendment.* This Agreement sets forth the entire understanding of the parties with respect to the subject matter
hereof and may not be changed, modified or terminated
except upon a written amendment executed by the Chairper-

son of the Employer and the Employee. Furthermore and without limitation, nothing in this Agreement shall be construed as giving the Employee any right to be retained in the employ of the Employer beyond the expiration of the Employment Term, and if employed thereafter the Employee specifically acknowledges that, unless the Employer and the Employee have either extended this Agreement by a written instrument or entered into a new, written employment agreement, he/she shall be an employee-at-will and thus subject to discharge with or without cause and without further compensation of any nature.

14.2 **Assignment.** All of the provisions of this Agreement shall be binding upon and inure to the benefit of and be enforceable by the respective heirs, executors, administrators, personal representatives, successors and assigns of the parties hereto, except that the duties and responsibilities of the Employee hereunder are of a personal nature and shall not be assignable or delegable in whole or in part by the Employee.

15.0 **Severability.** If any provision of this Agreement or the application thereof to anyone or any circumstance is held invalid or unenforceable in any jurisdiction, the remainder of this Agreement, and the application of such provision to such person or entity or such circumstance in any other jurisdiction or to other persons, entities or circumstances in any jurisdiction, shall not be affected thereby, and to this end the provisions of this Agreement are severable.

16.0 **Remedies Cumulative; No Waiver.** No remedy conferred upon any party by this Agreement is intended to be exclusive of any other remedy, and each and every such remedy shall be cumulative and in addition to any other remedy given hereunder or now or hereafter existing at law or in equity. No delay or omission by any party in exercising any right, remedy or power hereunder or existing at law or in equity shall be construed as a waiver thereof, and any such right, remedy or power may be exercised by such party from time to time and as often as may be deemed expedient or necessary by such party in its or his/her sole discretion.

17.0 *Miscellaneous.* This Agreement may be executed in several counterparts, each of which shall be an original. It shall not be necessary in making proof of this Agreement or any counterpart hereof to produce or account for any of the other counterparts.

IN WITNESS WHEREOF, the Employer and the Employee have executed this Agreement as of the date first above written.

[Corporate Seal]   XYZ COMPANY

Attest: _____   By: _____
       (Secretary)   (As its Chairperson)

                                        EMPLOYEE

_____   _____
      (Witness)   (JOHN/JANE DOE)

_____   _____
      (Date)   (Date)

Sample (1996) by Stephen J. Hirschfeld, a partner with McKenna & Cuneo, L.L.P., San Francisco, CA; 415/267-4127.

Separation Agreement and General Release

1.0   The intent of this Separation Agreement and General Release (hereinafter "Release") is to mutually, amicably and finally resolve and compromise all issues and claims of [NAME OF EMPLOYEE] (hereinafter "[USE LAST NAME OF EMPLOYEE]") employment with [NAME OF EMPLOYER] (hereinafter "COMMUNITY COLLEGE") and the separation thereof. EMPLOYEE will be separated from his employment with the COMMUNITY COLLEGE effective _____. The execution of this Release shall not in any way be considered an admission of any liability on the part of the COMMUNITY COLLEGE.

2.0   In exchange for the Release described below, the COMMUNITY COLLEGE agrees to:

   a.   The COMMUNITY COLLEGE will tender monies to EM-PLOYEE on _____ in the amount of _____, less legally-mandated payroll reductions and withholdings. This sum does not include any accrued, unused vacation pay which, if due and owing, shall also be tendered to EMPLOYEE on _____, less legally-mandated payroll reductions and withholdings.

   b.   [Optional: The COMMUNITY COLLEGE will continue to provide health insurance coverage to EMPLOYEE at no cost to him under the COMMUNITY COLLEGE'S regular plan for _____ months. Effective _____, EMPLOYEE may elect to continue health insurance coverage under the COMMU-NITY COLLEGE'S plan pursuant to the Consolidated Omnibus Budget Reconciliation Act.]

3.0   In consideration for the payments, promises, and undertakings described above, EMPLOYEE, his/her representatives, successors, and assigns do hereby completely release and forever discharge the COMMUNITY COLLEGE, officers, directors and trustees, and all other representatives, agents, directors, employees, attorneys, successors and assigns from all claims, rights, demands, actions, obligations, and causes of action of any and every kind, nature and character, known or unknown, which EMPLOYEE may now have, or has ever had, against them arising from or in any way connected with the employment relationship between the parties, any actions during the relationship, and/or the termination thereof, including, but not limited to, all "wrongful discharge" claims; and all claims relating to any contract of employment, express or implied; any covenant of good faith and fair dealing, express or implied; any tort of any nature; any federal, state, or municipal statute or ordinance; any claims under Title VII of the Civil Rights Act of 1964, the Civil Rights Act of 1991, the Age Discrimination in Employment Act, the Older Workers' Benefit Protection Act, 42 U.S.C. § 1981, the Employee Retirement and Income Security Act, the Americans with Disabilities Act, [add all applicable state and local laws], and any other laws and regulations relating to wages, benefits and employment discrimination and any and all claims for attorneys' fees and costs.

4.0   [Add if in California] EMPLOYEE has read Section 1542 of the Civil Code of the State of California, which provides as follows:

> A GENERAL RELEASE DOES NOT EXTEND TO CLAIMS WHICH THE CREDITOR DOES NOT KNOW OR SUSPECT TO EXIST IN HIS FAVOR AT THE TIME OF EXECUTING THE RELEASE, WHICH IF KNOWN BY HIM MUST HAVE MATERIALLY AFFECTED HIS SETTLEMENT WITH THE DEBTOR.

EMPLOYEE understands that Section 1542 gives him/her the right not to release existing claims of which he/she is not aware, unless he/she voluntarily chooses to waive his/her right. Having been so apprised, he/she nevertheless hereby voluntarily elects to, and does, waive the rights described in Section 1542, and elects to assume all risks for claims that now exist in his/her favor, known or unknown, from the subjects of this Release.

5.0   EMPLOYEE agrees that the existence of this Release and the existence of and terms and conditions of this Release are strictly confidential. EMPLOYEE also agrees to use his/her best efforts to prevent any publicity or disclosure of the facts, terms, and/or surrounding circumstances of this Release. If asked about the matter, he/she will only state that "it was resolved."

6.0 [**Optional:** EMPLOYEE and the COMMUNITY COLLEGE agree that in the event any taxing authority determines these monies to be taxable, EMPLOYEE is solely responsible for the payment of all such taxes and penalties assessed against him/her, except for legally mandated employer contributions, and that the COMMUNITY COLLEGE has no duty to defend EMPLOYEE against any such tax claim, penalty or assessment. EMPLOYEE agrees to cooperate in the defense of any such claim brought against the COMMUNITY COLLEGE. The COMMUNITY COLLEGE agrees to cooperate in defense of any such claim brought against EMPLOYEE.]

7.0 [**Optional — use if employee is 40 or older:** EMPLOYEE acknowledges that he/she has consulted with his/her attorney prior to signing the Release. Pursuant to the Older Workers Benefit Protection Act, EMPLOYEE has twenty-one (21) days in which to consider whether he/she should sign this Release; and if he/she signs this Release, he/she will have seven (7) days following the date on which he/she signs the Release to revoke it and the Release will not be effective until after this seven-day period has lapsed.]

8.0 In the event any controversy or dispute arises in connection with the validity, construction, application, enforcement or breach of this Separation Agreement and General Release, any such controversy or dispute shall be submitted to **final and binding arbitration** pursuant to the rules of the American Arbitration Association and the United States Arbitration Act and the parties hereto expressly waive their rights, if any, to have any such matters heard by a court or a jury, or administrative agency, whether state or federal. The arbitrator shall require the losing party to reimburse the prevailing party for reasonable attorneys' fees and costs incurred in connection with the arbitration. The losing party also shall be required to pay the arbitrator's fees for said arbitration.

9.0 This Release constitutes the entire understanding of the parties on the subjects covered. EMPLOYEE expressly warrants that he/she has read and fully understands this Release; that he/she has had the opportunity to consult with legal counsel of his/her own choosing and to have the terms of this Release fully explained to him/her, that he/she is not executing this Release in reliance on any promises, representations or inducements other than those contained herein; and that he/she is executing this Release voluntarily, free of any duress or coercion.

10.0 This Release shall be construed and governed by the laws of the State of [insert applicable state]. The parties hereto further agree that if, for any reason, any provisions hereof are unenforceable, the remainder of this Release shall nonetheless remain binding and in effect.

_____   _____
(Date)   (EMPLOYEE)

_____   _____
(Date)   (NAME OF COMMUNITY COLLEGE)

Sample (1996) by Stephen J. Hirschfeld, a partner with McKenna & Cuneo, L.L.P., San Francisco, CA; 415/267-4127.

BIBLIOGRAPHY AND RESOURCES

Appleberry, J. B. (1988). Checklist for a president's contract. *Association of Governing Boards Reports, 30*(2), 22–24.

Appleberry, J. B. (1996). *The presidential search and condition of employment.* Washington, DC: American Association of State Colleges and Universities.

Compensation, benefits, and conditions of employment for college and university chief executives. (1991). Washington, DC: College and University Personnel Association.

Creal, R. C., Beyer, K. D., & The Brookings Institution. (1995). *Administrative compensation survey.* Washington, DC: College and University Personnel Association.

Dowdy, H. (1987). *Manual for trustees of the North Carolina community college system.* Raleigh, NC: North Carolina State Department of Community Colleges.

Duryea, E. D., & Grossman, M. B. (1983). College and university government: West Chester State College. *Academe, 69*(3), 53–63.

Fisher, J. L. (1991). Presidential evaluation (review). In *The board and the president.* (pp. 72–79). New York: American Council on Education and Macmillan Publishing Company.

Koltai, L. (1984, April). *Strengthening the presidency.* Paper presented at the Annual Convention of the American Association of Community and Junior Colleges, Washington, DC.

Madden, J. S. (1991). *Annual benchmark compensation study for administrative positions* (Management Report 1990–91/2). Sacramento, CA: Association of California Community College Administrators.

Neff, C. B. (1994). What's in a presidential contract? *Association of Governing Boards Trusteeship, 2*(1), 26–27, 34.

Ness, F. W., & Miller, B. (1988). Presidential removal: biting the bullet. *Association of Governing Boards Reports, 30*(6), 15–19.

Nicholson, R. S. (1981). *Chief executive officers: contracts and compensation.* Washington, DC: American Association of Community and Junior Colleges.

Nicholson, R. S. (1988). *Chief executive officers: contracts and compensation.* Washington, DC: American Association of Community and Junior Colleges.

Parnell, D., & Rivera, M. (1991). *College chief executive officers' contracts, salaries, and compensation.* Washington, DC: American Association of Community and Junior Colleges.

Peat Marwick/AS&U compensation survey part II: For college & university executives. (1985). *American School and University, 57*(7), 36–38,43–44, 46, 51–52, 54, 56, 60, 62.

Peat Marwick/AS&U compensation survey part II: For college & university executives. (1986). *American School and University, 57*(7), 36–38, 43–44, 46, 51–52, 54, 56, 60, 62.

Seldin, P. (1988). How to evaluate campus executives. *Association of Governing Boards Reports, 30*(5), 16–19.

Simerly, R., & Prisk, D. (1992). Negotiating employment contracts for CEOs in continuing education: Practical tips and advice based on researching professional practice. *The Journal of Continuing Higher Education, 40*(2), 14–25.

Strider, R. E. (1982). Checking out presidential assessment. *Association of Governing Boards Reports, 24*(1), 54–56.

Vanderheyden, B. (1994). *Salaries of administrators in the North Carolina community college system* (Research brief No. 1994-04). Raleigh, NC: North Carolina State Department of Community Colleges.

AACC PRESIDENTS ACADEMY EXECUTIVE COMMITTEE

APPENDIX A

JULY 1, 1995–JUNE 30, 1996

Karen A. Bowyer
Chair
President, Dyersburg State Community College
Dyersburg, Tennessee

Ruth Mercedes Smith
Chair-elect
President, Highland Community College
Freeport, Illinois

Ronald K. Lingle
Immediate Past Chair
President, Coastal Carolina Community College
Jacksonville, North Carolina

Julius R. Brown
Southern Representative
President, Wallace Community College
Selma, Alabama

David L. Buettner
Central Representative
President, North Iowa Area Community College
Mason City, Iowa

Charles R. Dassance
Central Representative
President, Ashland Community College
Ashland, Kentucky

Deborah M. DiCroce
Southern Representative
President, Piedmont Virginia Community College
Charlottesville, Virginia

Tommy Lewis, Jr.
Pacific Representative
Navajo Community College
Tsaile, Arizona

Eduardo J. Marti
Northern Representative
President, Corning Community College
Corning, New York

Jo Anne Y. McFarland
Western Representative
President, Central Wyoming College
Riverton, Wyoming

Queen F. Randall
Pacific Representative
Chancellor, Los Rios Community College District
Sacramento, California

Martha A. Smith
Northern Representative
President, Anne Arundel Community College
Arnold, Maryland

Carol J. Spencer
Western Representative
President, Cedar Valley College
Lancaster, Texas

STAFF CONTACT:

Carrole A. Wolin
AACC Director of Professional Development

EX-OFFICIO:

David R. Pierce
AACC President & CEO

Daniel F. Moriarty
Chair, AACC Board of Directors

RESPONDENTS PER STATE BY REGION

APPENDIX B

REGIONS	RESPONDENTS
CENTRAL:	
Illinois	36
Indiana	2
Iowa	12
Kentucky	11
Michigan	17
Minnesota	12
Missouri	14
Ohio	21
Wisconsin	11
NORTHERN:	
Connecticut	7
Delaware	1
Maine	5
Maryland	10
Massachusetts	14
New Hampshire	3
New Jersey	12
New York	28
Pennsylvania	17
Rhode Island	0
Vermont	2
PACIFIC:	
Alaska	2
Arizona	9
California	59
Hawaii	1
Micronesia	2
Nevada	1
Oregon	12
Utah	3
Washington	17

REGIONS	RESPONDENTS
SOUTHERN:	
Alabama	13
Arkansas	12
Florida	17
Georgia	16
Louisiana	2
Mississippi	12
North Carolina	40
South Carolina	13
Tennessee	8
Virginia	21
West Virginia	5
WESTERN:	
Colorado	7
Idaho	4
Kansas	18
Montana	2
Nebraska	4
New Mexico	7
North Dakota	4
Oklahoma	10
South Dakota	2
Texas	33
Wyoming	5

Note: Twenty-one respondents did not report their state.